PACIFIC SLOPE
RAILROADS

RAILROADS

FROM 1854 TO 1900

BY

GEORGE B. ABDILL

DAYS OF GLORY on old Glorieta Mountain are recaptured by this photo taken in the pinelands of New Mexico's Glorieta Pass in 1880. The husky, polished Consolidation is Baldwin-built No. 137 of the Atchison, Topeka & Santa Fe, affectionately called the BABY by her proud crew. This section of the Santa Fe road was constructed by the New Mexico & Southern Pacific Railroad, a subsidiary company organized by the Santa Fe. (Courtesy of Santa Fe Railway)

BONANZA BOOKS : NEW YORK

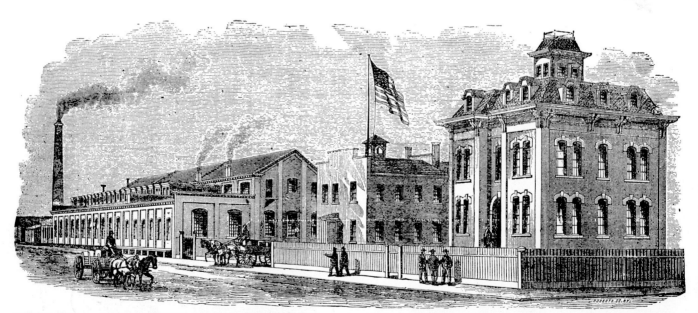

THE SCHENECTADY LOCOMOTIVE WORKS

Continue to receive orders, and to furnish with promptness the best and latest Improved

COAL OR WOOD BURNING LOCOMOTIVE ENGINES,

And other Railroad Machinery, Tires, etc., etc., and also to Repair and Rebuild Locomotives.

The above Works, located on the N. Y. C. R. R., near the centre of the State, possess superior facilities for forwarding work to any part of the country.

WALTER McQUEEN, Superintendent.   **CHAS. G. ELLIS, Treasurer.**   **JOHN C. ELLIS, President.**

Dedication.

For My Son

Daniel Bruce Abdill

who was born too late to witness

the Golden Age of Steam Railroading

Foreword.

THE reader who seeks the smooth flow of the professional writer in this work is doomed to disappointment. It is not a literary effort, but rather a collection of stories gathered in cabs, cabooses, and along the iron pike by a working locomotive engineer. The histories and information regarding the various lines have been checked for accuracy but even the experts are not in agreement on some details, and the records of various railroad companies have been found to contain errors.

The author has attempted to recapture, through the wonderful medium of the camera, the glory that was railroading in the western United States. From the collections of railroad historians, museums, individuals, and the archives of railroad companies a group of photographs has been selected to give the reader a pictorial glimpse of the steam locomotive and its crew in the wonderful era when the steel rails were bringing growth and progress to the region west of the Rocky Mountains. The result of this attempt is a panoramic vignette of railroading in the American West from the 1850's to the start of the present century, a photographic record of engines, trains, wrecks, and railroad scenes that could have passed before the eye of a boomer engineer rooling over the historic roads of the region.

For the use of the rare photographs included in the book, the writer is indebted to numerous sources. Fred Jukes, Ben Griffiths, Ronald V. Nixon, and Henry R. Griffiths, Jr., must receive special thanks for their contributions of pictures and data. The section devoted to the lines of California and the Southwest have been made possible through the generous cooperation of David L. Joslyn, G. M. Best, Roy D. Graves, R. P. Middlebrook, Mr. J. G. Shea of the Southern Pacific, and Mr. H. P. O'Leary of the Santa Fe.

The writer is grateful to Kate B. Carter, president of the Central Company, Daughter of Utah Pioneers, and to Earl Olson, Librarian, Latter-day Saints Church, for photos and information on the pioneer roads of the Salt Lake region, and to Mel Hanna of Roseburg, Oregon, for the use of valuable early rail maps.

Special thanks are due the following for their aid in providing pictures: David L. Stearns, John T. Labbe, Jack Slattery, H. L. Goldsmith, Lloyd Graham, El White, C. Walt Mendenhall, Ed Wiwatowski, Ronnie Hughes, Guy Dunscomb, Benj. T. Hart, Joe Williamson, Ralph Andrews, Jesse Ebert, Arthur M. Sayre, Gilbert Kneiss, Fred Fellow, Arthur Petersen, and a host of other individuals, including Jay Golden, who lent his personal attention to much of the photo copying.

Mrs. Irene A. Keeffe of the Union Pacific Historical Museum, E. C. Schafer of the Union Pacific Railroad, A. D. Collier of Collier State Park Logging Museum, Chas. E. Fisher of the Railway & Locomotive Historical Society, and N. J. Finigan of the Canadian Pacific Railway have all assisted greatly, along with the staff and curators of the Utah State Historical Society, Oregon Historical Society, State Historical Society of Colorado, and the Western Collection of the Denver Public Library.

PACIFIC SLOPE RAILROADS

In all of the colorful sagas of American railroading, the searcher would be hard put to find a more picturesque cross-section than that which existed west of the Rocky Mountains. Here the pioneer builders hacked out the primitive beginnings of rail lines that grew into transcontinental systems and a multitude of short lines bloomed and then withered away. The region was one of striking contrasts, ranging from rugged mountains to lush valleys to barren deserts.

The railroaders who toiled over the western land encountered a multitude of problems and troubles. They chilled in the great snowfalls that blanketed the mountain ranges to an unbelievable depth and they perspired in the blazing heat of the arid deserts. Their engines whistled through the gloomy aisles of rocky canyons and clattered through scenes of pastoral wealth and beauty. The smoke plumes from their locomotives drifted through the spars of ocean vessels anchored at terminals on the Pacific shore, and the steam exhaust wafted through the giant trees of virgin forests.

Beauty and Death walked hand in hand across this vast domain, constant companions of the crews who labored up the heartbreaking grades and sped along the level tangents. Flash floods sluiced the desert arroyos, tumbling bridges like so many matchsticks . . . torrential rains sent massive slides of rock, earth, and trees to block the iron trails threading the hill country. Raging fires swept the forests, consuming trestles and stations in awful fury, and coastal fogs blanketed the landscape with a wooly cover that watchful eyes strained to penetrate.

Bravely the crews fared forth into these dangers, rolling their primitive trains along the puny tracks that led to places with names that lay like music on the land . . . Needles and Barstow and Ask Fork . . . Colfax and Reno

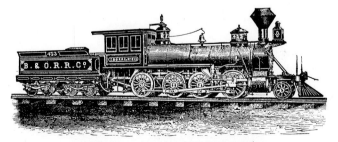

and Carline . . . Wallula, now only a memory buried beneath the waters of the Columbia . . . Huntington and Pocatello and Ogden . . . Wenatchee and Pasco and Spokane . . . Missoula, Butte, San Berdoo and 'Frisco. Defying the hazards and elements, boomer and homeguard alike stuck to their post and rode their smoking iron steeds into the pages of Western history.

Not all of these unsung heroes survived the wild and carefree days . . . some were blown to glory from their wooden cabs, others cashed in when trains ran away or fell through bridges or crashed into each other in a fearful assortment of wrecks and accidents. Yet there are veterans grown grey in the service who remember when wood cinders erupted from diamond stacks, when thirty cars was a huge train, and when the railroad man occupied a position of esteem and prestige in his community. These ancients who survive can recall the grueling hours and the dangers of railroading, the battles fought by railroad labor to improve conditions and bring a measure of safety into their daily existence. No monuments proclaim their deeds, but the ribbons of steel that thread the land from the Rockies to the Pacific bear witness of their passing.

To those who served so faithfully and to their women who loved and waited for them, the American West owes an everlasting debt of gratitude.

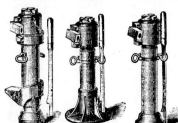

Table of Contents.

THE FIRST LOCOMOTIVE IN CALIFORNIA was this inside-connected 4-4-0 built by the Globe Locomotive Works of Boston in 1849. Shipped around Cape Horn to San Francisco in 1854, she carried the name ELEPHANT, and was used by Commodore C. K. Garrison in leveling sand dunes around the Bay City. Renamed the C. K. GARRISON, she was taken up to the pioneer Sacramento Valley Railroad as their No. 4, later becoming their second No. 1. In 1868 she was renamed PIONEER and was scrapped by the Central Pacific in 1886. Note the odd circular steam chests with their tallow cup lubricators. (Courtesy of Southern Pacific)

1

Rails East.

The pages of American history are rife with exciting deeds and colorful spectacles, from Washington crossing the Delaware to Custer's gory finish, but few of these stirring episodes can rival the simple ceremony enacted on a sage-covered flat north of the Great Salt Lake on May 10th, 1869. Two locomotives, each with polished brass gleaming, edged toward each other and halted just short of a gap in the track. Ties, including one of polished California laurel, were laid in place, and two lengths of rail fitted across them. After a prayer and a few fitting remarks, two gold and two silver spikes were presented and set into holes prepared to receive them. At a signal, silver spike mauls descended and the nation's first transcontinental railroad was connected.

GOVERNOR STANFORD, the first locomotive of the Central Pacific Rail Road Company of California, was named in honor of Leland Stanford, a New York farm boy who rose to fame as Governor of the State of California and the first president of the Central Pacific. The engine was originally built to 5 foot gauge by R. Norris & Son of Philadelphia in 1862, but was converted to standard gauge shortly after erection. Her dimensions included 15 x 22 inch cylinders, 54 inch drivers and 100 pounds of working pressure in her brass-bound boiler. First used in constuction, she was later relegated to yard and shop switching, underwent a re-building, and was then laid aside as unserviceable. In the late 1890's the veteran was taken into the Sacramento Shops, restored, and placed on permanent display at Stanford University, an institution founded by Gov. Stanford as a memorial to his only son, Leland Stanford Jr., who died shortly before his sixteenth birthday. (Courtesy of Southern Pacific)

THIRD LOCOMOTIVE ON THE CENTRAL PACIFIC was built by Danforth, Cooke & Company in 1863. The little 4-2-4 was named the C. P. HUNTINGTON in honor of Collis Potter Huntington, the driving force of the "Big Four." This early view shows the engine as she originally appeared during construction of the road. She later became No. 1 of the Southern Pacific, then was renumbered 1001. As the years passed the little kettle that had rounded the Horn aboard the sailing ship SUCCESS grew too light for regular service, but was fitted out and used as a weed burner. In later years she was restored, renumbered Southern Pacific No. 1, and re-tired on permanent display at the Sacramento depot. The Southern Pacific recently moved a huge 4-8-8-2 cab-in-fronter into the park as a companion to the first steam engine used on their road, creating an exhibit of striking contrast. (Courtesy of Southern Pacific)

The momentous occasion was witnessed by a motley crowd that included powerful railroad nabobs and humble working stiffs, Army officers and Chinese coolies, yet the man who visualized this event and was responsible to a great degree for the project was not there to see the hour of triumph. Theodore Dehone Judah had been dead for six years, but his spirit surely must have rejoiced as the two engines moved ahead and touched pilots, fulfilling Judah's great vision of a steel highway stretching from the Atlantic to the Pacific.

Theodore D. Judah, born in Connecticut in 1826, was a trained civil engineer and came west to California in 1854 to survey the pioneer Sacramento Valley Railroad. While employed on this and subsequent rail projects, Judah never ceased to dream of a "Great Pacific Railroad", dwelling so much on the subject that he was sometimes called "Crazy" Judah. The thought of a railroad over the Sierra and across the desolate wastelands to some eastern terminal was practically beyond the comprehension of many Californians.

Judah agitated for a Pacific Railroad project constantly, going to Washington, D. C., in 1859 to arouse interest in the national capitol. In 1860, he was back in the California mountains, scouting out feasible routes for a railway. The best of these appeared to be the Dutch Flat route, crossing over the Sierra Nevada through Donner Pass, site of the terrible privations suffered by the ill-fated Donner party of emigrants.

Encouraged by Dr. Daniel Strong, a Dutch Flat dentist, Judah worked up a proposed route, complete with engineering data, and, with Strong, set about securing stock subscriptions. After a number of meetings, the stockholders organized the Central Pacific Railroad Company on June 28th, 1861. By October of that year, Judah had completed a more extensive survey and was sent back to Washington to campaign for support from the Federal Government. A bill to provide this assistance was signed into law by President Lincoln on July 1st, 1862, and Judah made a trip to New York to order supplies and equipment. He departed for California on July 21st and the dream he had cherished was about to blossom. The directors of the Central Pacific Railroad had gradually dropped out until the affairs of the company rested principally in the hands of four men, all destined to rise to fame through the medium of Judah's vision. These four, prosperous California merchants, were Leland Stanford, Collis P. Huntington, Charles Crocker, and Mark Hopkins.

On January 8th, 1863, ground for the first transcontinental railway was broken at Sacramento, but the "Big Four", as the above-named directors were known, soon disagreed with Judah and a split came about. The partners purchased Judah's interest for $100,000 and the disgruntled engineer headed east to attempt to gain new backing, possibly from the Vanderbilts. Crossing the Isthmus of Panama, the unfortunate Judah contracted yellow fever. He reached New York on October 28th, 1863, and in a few days succumbed to his illness. Death came for Judah when he was not quite thirty-eight years of age, but the recognition of his efforts are permanently engraved upon the pages of Ameri-

FIRST MAJOR STREAM encountered by the Central Pacific was the American River, just out of Sacramento. The original span is shown here, with the locomotive C. P. HUNTINGTON at the right. The bridge consisted of two Howe trusses set on piling piers, these piers later being replaced with stone masonry. The two wooden spans, later destroyed by fire, covered a distance of 400 feet; the trestle approach from the Sacramento side was 2,196 feet long and the trestle at the north end of the span was 2,890 feet long, making the total length of spans and approaches 5,486 feet, over a mile in length. The trestling at each end carried the tracks over the low bottomlands that often flooded in stages of high water. (Courtesy of Southern Pacific)

CENTRAL PACIFIC'S ENGINE NO. 4 was built by Danforth, Cooke & Co. in 1864 and bore the name T. D. JUDAH, in honor of Theodore Dehone Judah, Central Pacific's first Chief Engineer and the man who envisioned the Pacific Railway. Originally a 4-2-4 and a sister of the C. P. HUNTINGTON, the JUDAH was rebuilt into a 4-2-2 type with a separate tender and later was sold to the Wellington Colliery Company in British Columbia. This rare photo from the Southern Pacific archives shows not only the locomotive as rebuilt, but includes the shadow of the photographer and his tripod mounted wet plate camera of heroic dimensions. (Courtesy of Southern Pacific)

can history. More than any other man, his was the dream that sparked the Pacific Railroad into existence.

The task that confronted the builders of the new Central Pacific was of such Herculean magnitude as to defy any but the stoutest of heart. When T. D. Judah died, Samuel S. Montague was appointed acting chief engineer, later being appointed chief engineer on March 31st, 1868. The first contract, let to Charles Crocker in December, 1862, was for the first eighteen miles of road, including the bridge over the American River. The first rail was laid in Sacramento on October 26th, 1863, and the road's first locomotive, the *Governor Stanford,* was placed in operation on November 10th of the same year.

The road had to be built to Government specifications, including the use of American rails, and the Crocker contract was divided into sections, with portions assigned to sub-contractors. These included Truxton, Knox, and Ryan; C. D. Bates; Cyrus Collins & Brother, and S. B. Smith. It was not until June 10th, 1864, that the first 31 miles to Newcastle were placed in operation. This had been

an easy portion, the line crossing level country with only minor construction problems. The real job lay ahead, for the work grew progressively heavier as the grade started the tough conquest of the Sierras.

Money was scant in the Central Pacific treasury, and the Civil War, raging in the East and South, skyrocketed the cost of supplies and equipment. Added to the inflated initial costs was the expensive freight charges, for practically all of the manufactured equipment had to be shipped around Cape Horn or transported across the Isthmus of Panama.

The road's first locomotive, the *Governor Stanford,* came around Cape Horn on the sailing vessel, *Herald of the Morning,* and was shipped up to Sacramento from San Francisco on the schooner *Anna R. Forbes.* She was unloaded on the Sacramento levee and came very nearly being lost in the river in the process. The engine cost the Central Pacific the sum of $13,688, of which $2,282 were freight charges; before the start of the Civil War an engine of the *Stanford* type could be purchased for about $7,500.

As the crews pushed the track rapidly eastward, the motive power situation became so desperate that two new engines, manufactured in the East, were dismantled and hauled across the Isthmus of Panama. This cost the road about $8,000 in freight charges for each of the two locomotives. The cost of black powder for blasting jumped from $2.50 to $15.00 per keg.

The first engines used on the road were quite light, the No. 3, *C P. Huntington,* being capable of handling about four cars weighing 22 tons each on a slight grade. To meet the increased demand for heavier loads, the Central Pacific ordered a 4-6-0 from the Mason Manufacturing Company, and this locomotive was tried out on March 16th, 1865. She was No. 6, named the *Conness,* and was reputed to be the most powerful engine on the Pacific Coast at the time of her maiden trip.

With bigger and better power, the work trains kept supplies rolling up to the end of track. By September of 1865 the road reached what is now known as Colfax and the grading became increasingly difficult. A wage strike by Irish grading gangs was broken by the introduction of large numbers of Chinese, and these proved so adapted to the task that more and more Oriental laborers were employed. At one time, about 12,000 Chinese were at work on the Central Pacific. One of these, Ah Jim by name, passed away at his home in Live Oak, California, in 1945. Reputed to be 118 years old, he was the last known survivor of any of the men employed in the construction of the road across the Sierra. When the railway was finished, most of the Chinese turned to mining, gardening, and other tasks, scattering throughout the West. Many of them became excellent cooks and were in demand in restaurants and ranch kitchens, as well as in logging camps, while nearly every Western village of any size boasted at least one Chinese laundry.

When the rails began to thread the granite walls of the Sierra Nevada, the task of tunneling began in earnest. In the twenty miles of track between Cisco and the summit it was necessary to drill nine bores totaling 5,158 feet. Most of the blasting was done with black powder, but at Tunnel 6 the use of nitroglycerine was inaugurated. James Howden was employed to manufacture this potent explosive at the tunnel site.

The winter of 1866-67 was so severe that most work on the mountain section was brought to a standstill. Over 44 feet of snow fell, and still the crews labored, retreating inside the mountain to excavate tunnels until the advent of warm weather would clear the way for more track work. A small locomotive was dismantled, taken up to Gold Run,

BLOOMER CUT, a narrow defile through a conglomerate formation of cement gravel, had to be blasted out to make a path for the Central Pacific's rails. This cut, about 800 feet long and some 65 feet deep, was located west of Auburn, California. Here a Central Pacific locomotive, tank piled high with wood, heads a train of construction supplies through the sheer walls of the gap. (Courtesy of Southern Pacific)

and loaded on a wide-wheeled truck. Ten yoke of oxen yarded this monstrous burden through Cisco to the Summit, where it was used as a stationary engine on the big tunnel. Crews were grading and boring in from each end of this tunnel, but the work went so slowly that a center shaft was sunk, a hoisting engine powered by the dismantled locomotive placed in service, and the tunneling was carried on from four faces.

Snow slides swept away construction camps and buried a number of workmen, but the men of the

15

ENGINE NO. 5 of the Central Pacific was built by the Mason Manufacturing Company in 1864 and was named the ATLANTIC. She had 15 x 22 inch cylinders, weighed 58,000 pounds, and bore Mason's Shop Number 145. In later years she became No. 1006 of the Southern Pacific and was scrapped in 1894.

HEAVIEST ENGINE ON THE COAST at the time of her arrival, Central Pacific's No. 6 was a 4-6-0 built by William Mason in 1864 and shipped around Cape Horn to California. Named the CONNESS, she was the first ten-wheeler owned by the road. No. 6 had 48 inch drivers, 17 x 24 inch cylinders, and weighed 70,500 pounds. She ended her days as Southern Pacific's No. 2000, being scrapped in 1908.

NATIVE DAUGHTER OF THE BEAR STATE, Central Pacific's No. 7, the A. A. SARGENT, was the third locomotive built by Booth & Company of San Francisco. Constructed in 1865, she was named for a California politico, United States Senator A. A. Sargent, who aided T. D. Judah in obtaining passage of the Pacific Railroad measures. This photo, taken in 1865, shows the engine standing at the foot of K Street in Sacramento; at right is the historic old Brannan House, early-day hostelry.

Central Pacific were not to be deterred. Several locomotives were loaded on sleighs or log sleds and carted down the eastern face of the Sierra into the Truckee Canyon, where light snowfall made it possible to lay track. In addition to the three locomotives, the crews sledded forty cars and enough rail for forty miles of track over twenty-eight miles of the roughest mountain trails one can imagine to advance the work. Considering that this was accomplished under staggering obstacles, the job of transporting this equipment must rank high in the annals of human achievement.

Work on the track in the mountains was renewed in June of 1867 and the end of track reached the summit in November of that year. In the summer of 1867, the first experimental snowsheds and galleries were constructed, since the old wedge-type snow plows in use at that time could not combat the huge drifts that blocked the line in winter. These sheds proved so practical that over 40 miles of them were erected to protect the road.

However, it was impractical to cover the entire route over the Sierra with snowsheds, and a select group of locomotive engineers were regularly assigned to buck the drifts on the unprotected sections of the line. Among these early throttle artists who earned the title of "The Storm Kings" were Engineers Spence, Daily, Hawkins, and others. With five to seven engines coupled behind a wedge plow, these experts battered away at snow drifts that were

as much as 20 feet in depth, backing down and charging ahead until they finally forced their way through. It was hazardous work, but the mountain men thrilled to the challenge and held themselves to be a notch or two above their brother runners in the valley.

With the advantage given by the snowsheds, the track gangs were able to keep the line open, assisted by the wedge plows.

The new road was opened into Reno, Nevada, on the 19th of June, 1868, and the race against the Union Pacific got under way in earnest. On July 22nd of 1868, the trains were running into Wadsworth, Nevada, located at the Big Bend of the Truckee River. Wadsworth became an important terminal until a line relocation in later years left it marooned on a branch.

Grading and track laying was rushed through the summer of 1868, the work of grading through Palisade Canyon being done far in advance of the end of track. Hay, grain, supplies, and water had to be freighted for long distances to keep these advance grading gangs supplied. The winter of 1868-69 was one of freezing cold, the ground in the valley of the upper reaches of the Humboldt becoming frozen to a depth of several feet. Handling the grading through this frozen earth by ordinary methods was impossible, and it had to be blasted and treated in the same fashion as rock.

The locomotives in use on the road at this time

FIRST MOGUL TYPE purchased by the Central Pacific was No. 8, the NEVADA. The locomotive and two sister 2-6-0's, No. 9, the UTAH and No. 10, the HUMBOLDT, were built by Danforth, Cooke & Company in 1865. The management of the road was not favorably impressed with the Mogul wheel arrangement and the engines were converted to other types, the NEVADA reportedly becoming a 4-6-0. (Courtesy of Southern Pacific)

CENTRAL PACIFIC'S NO 25 was the second engine on the road to bear that number. She was acquired from the old original Western Pacific Railroad to replace the former No. 25, destroyed in an accident. Built by J. A. Norris of Lancaster, Pennsylvania, in 1864, she was lettered "I" and named the INDUSTRY while in service on the Western Pacific; originally burning wood, she is reputed to have been the first locomotive in California to use coal for fuel. (Courtesy of Southern Pacific)

were all burning wood, and as the track reached across the desert, the problem of fuel supply mounted. Wood for the locomotives, as well as ties and bridge timbers, came from the timbered slopes of the Truckee River and had to be forwarded by rail to the terminals far out on the barren plains of Nevada.

In addition to Samuel S. Montague, the Central Pacific had a number of able civil engineers engaged in location. These included Lewis M. Clement, who located the line around the cliff known as Cape Horn; the tracks here were on a ledge hacked from stone, with a sheer drop of 1,200 feet from the roadbed to the waters of the American River in the canyon below.

The superintendent in charge of actual construction under Charles Crocker was James H. Strowbridge, a Vermonter known for his strong will and ready flow of profanity. Strowbridge and his wife lived in a box car, moving east as the rails advanced. The Union Pacific construction camps were wild and wide open, the workers preyed upon by gamblers, prostitutes, and saloon keepers, but the Central Pacific was notably lacking in this rough element. The credit for much of this orderliness is due to Strowbridge, for he hated liquor and took the law into his own hands, destroying tents and liquor supplies of those who tried to serve the men in his crews. Then, too, the large numbers of Chin-

ese employed kept to themselves, shunning strong drink and limiting their gambling to fan-tan games, thus contributing to the peaceful nature of Strowbridge's operations.

The extensive bridge work on the road was in charge of Arthur Brown, a Scot from Kentore, near Aberdeen. He supervised the construction of buildings as well as bridges, remaining with the road long after completion of the original line. When the wooden truss bridge over the American River at Sacramento was destroyed by fire, Brown and his force rebuilt the structure and had it in service forty hours after the job was started.

The grand climax of the Central Pacific saga came when the final spike connecting the line with the Union Pacific was sunk at Promontory, Utah, on May 10th, 1869. The event was celebrated throughout the land, although the ceremonies on the spot were rather simple. The various views of the wedding of the rails have been widely published, showing Engine 119 of the Union Pacific facing the funnel-stacked *Jupiter*, Central Pacific's No. 60. Actually, the Central Pacific's No. 29, a trim McKay & Aldus eight-wheeler named the *Antelope,* had started for the Promontory rites with Gov. Stanford's special train, but a blast in the Sierras put her out of commission and the *Jupiter* was pressed into service at Truckee to take over the honors.

Since no definite meeting point for the two rival roads had been designated by the Government, each line kept right on grading past the other, in some cases coming to battle as the competing grade gangs worked in the same vicinity. Roughly 200 miles of this parallel grading was done before a compromise was reached and the meeting point established at Promontory, the Central Pacific purchasing over 47 miles of completed Union Pacific trackage to carry them to a point 5 miles west of Ogden; this 5 mile segment was then leased from the Union Pacific for 999 years.

With the completion of the transcontinental railway, train service between the Atlantic and Pacific states was soon in effect, although passengers had to change cars at Promontory. The Union Pacific trains carried Pullman sleeping cars, but the Central Pacific operated their own sleeping car service. In June, 1869, the car building firm of Jackson & Sharp, located in Wilmington, Delaware, delivered the first of this company-owned rolling stock. Known as the Silver Palace Sleeping Cars, they were the latest word in comfort and appointment. The bodies were of wood, the interiors tastefully finished in bird's-eye maple and polished walnut. Red silk plush upholstery covered the seats and Brussels carpeting was spread over the floors. The cars were heated by coal stoves and illuminated by oil lamps or candles. The Central Pacific operated this fancy equipment until July 1st, 1883, when they transferred it all to the Pullman Palace Car Company.

In the early years of operation, even freight cars were not operated across the two roads, all freight being transferred from the cars of one line to that of the other at the Promontory junction, these operations later being shifted to the terminal at Ogden.

No dining cars were included in the early passenger trains, passengers being fed at eating houses located at various terminals. Schedules were arranged to allow time for dining at these various stops. It was not until around 1890 that the Pullman Company placed three dining cars in service between Ogden and Truckee. In 1894 the railroad purchased this equipment and has since operated its own dining car service.

In order to better serve the Pacific Coast, the road extended from Sacramento to San Francisco Bay by way of the old Western Pacific Railroad route, via Niles Canyon and Stockton. The famous ferry boat service delivered passengers from Oakland to San Francisco, the ride across the Bay being a memorable part of the journey that few travelers ever forgot.

The "Big Four," once the Central Pacific was completed, began to expand, and the Southern Pa-

PRIMITIVE MERRY-GO-'ROUND, this crude turntable of the Central Pacific was located at Newcastle, California. Engine No. 6, the CONNESS, is being turned in this photo taken in 1864. In the background, construction work is in progress; the timber trestle has been erected by bridge crews and one-horse dump carts are engaged in building the earthen fill up to grade. (Courtesy of Southern Pacific)

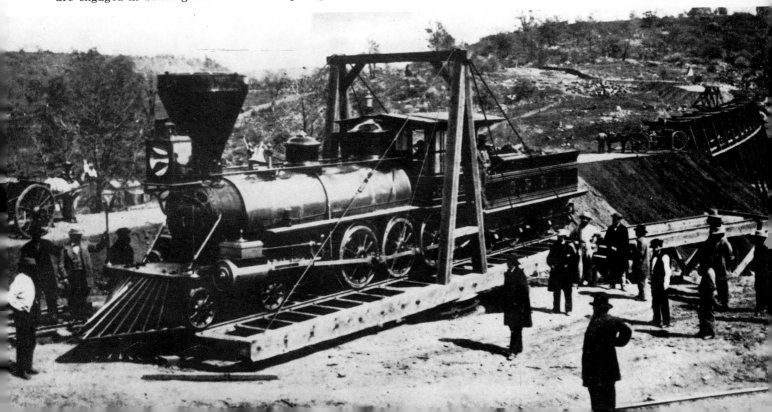

McKAY & ALDUS IRON WORKS, located in East Boston, Massachusetts, built this neat American Standard for the Central Pacific in 1867. The engine had 5-foot drivers, 16 x 24 inch cylinders, was assigned Road Number 28, and was named the GOLD RUN, after the mining community located west of Dutch Flat. She later became Southern Pacific's No. 1191 and was scrapped in 1898.

cific Railroad Company was organized to carry out their far-reaching plans. The famous "Sunset Route" struck off from the old main line at Lathrop, California, in December of 1869. Rails were laid through the San Joaquin Valley, reaching Sumner, now called East Bakersfield, in the fall of 1874. The next step was the climb over the Tehachapi Mountains, where a grade of 2. 2 per cent, 18 tunnels, and Engineer William Hood's famous loop were needed to carry the rails over this barrier. The line reached Mojave on August 8th, 1876. Construction was started both north and east out of Los Angeles in 1873, and the north line joined the extension south from Mojave through Soledad Canyon at Lang station, the last spike being driven there on September 5th, 1876.

East from the City of Angels, the road ran through Colton to Indian Wells, now known as Indio, crossing the vast desert and skirting the Salton Sea on its way to the Colorado River crossing at Yuma. The road reached Yuma in 1877 and terminated there until 1878, when construction was resumed and the line opened into Tucson, Arizona, on March 20th, 1880.

While the Central Pacific had encountered but little trouble with the Indians during construction of the Overland Route, the Southern Pacific line east was being built through Apache country, and much of the work was done under military escort. In spite of this added difficulty, the rails were opened for service to Lordsburg, New Mexico, on October 18th, 1880, and reached El Paso, Texas, on May 19th, 1881. By some rapid construction, the new Southern Pacific line beat the Texas &

Pacific into Sierra Blanca, then acquired a number of separate railroads to form a connection through to New Orleans, Louisiana.

Through construction and the acquisition of numerous short line railroads, the great Central Pacific-Southern Pacific network soon spread over the Pacific West. The road north to Oregon, originally called the California & Oregon Railroad, started work at Marysville in October of 1869, reaching Redding on September 1st, 1872, where the end of track was to remain for 12 years. Work north of Redding was resumed in the spring of 1883 and the end of track was soon in the tortuous canyon of the Sacramento River. In the course of construction through the canyon, 17 bridges were built to carry the rails over the winding Sacramento. The heavy masonry work in this region was done under the supervision of a Scotchman, Col. James Scobie.

Names made famous by the construction of the Central Pacific were again to appear in news items as the work on the Shasta Route progressed. Strowbridge, Montague, Crocker, and Brown, all veterans of the Overland project, were in command of the crews advancing north under the snowy peak of Mount Shasta. Chinese were used in large numbers, grading with pick, shovel, and wheelbarrow. Train and engine crews brought solid trains of construction material north from Sacramento, some of them being held at the end of track for additional work train service.

Under the eastern flank of the Trinity Mountains, the railroad established a camp on the banks of the Sacramento and named it Cedar Flat. A boxcar was set out and used to house the telegrapher and railroad office. Not long after the Cedar Flat station was established its name was changed to Dunsmuir, honoring the Scottish family prominent in the coal mines and business of British Columbia. Within a short time, the boxcar depot was moved up the line a short distance to a station formerly called Pusher, taking the name, Dunsmuir, with it. The railroad established a division point at the new location and erected a roundhouse to care for the woodburning locomotives being used on the road. The Hon. Robert Dunsmuir donated an ornamental fountain to the rail village named in honor of his family and the old fountain became one of the local landmarks, recalling the story of the boxcar station that grew into a busy railroad terminal.

North of Dunsmuir, the new road climbed the steep Cantara loops and passed through the station of Mott, California, named in honor of the first roadmaster on the Division. The line passed through Strawberry Valley and north to Edgewood, Gazelle, and Grenada to Montague, thence to Snowden and into Hornbrook. Ahead lay the rugged Siskiyou Mountains, requiring a great deal of tunnel building and so steep that the maximum grade ran up to 3.3 per cent.

The Oregon & California Railroad, built south from Portland to Ashland via Roseburg and Grants Pass, had reached the northern abutment of the Siskiyous at Ashland in 1884, but it was not until the 17th of December, 1887, that Charley Crocker hammered home the final spike linking the Oregon road with the line built north through the Shasta Wonderland.

Through the years, the locomotives of the Central Pacific-Southern Pacific increased in size; the tiny *C. P. Huntington* seemed little more than a toy

ROCKLIN ROUNDHOUSE was a stronghold of Central Pacific operations when this photograph was taken in 1868. The engine on the 55-foot turntable appears to be No. 45, the MAJESTIC. The huge piles of wood corded in the foreground are the fuel supply for the road's locomotives; when the Rogers 4-6-0 engines were in service in the 1880's, the fireman palmed an average of 16 cords of wood into the roaring firebox on the 82 mile run between Rocklin and Summit. The Rocklin terminal operations were transferred to Roseville in 1908. (Courtesy of Southern Pacific)

HEADED FOR THE FRONT, a rangy Mogul drags a string of flats across a high Central Pacific trestle near Newcastle, California. This timber structure was 528 feet in length. The 2-6-0, carrying construction materials to the end of track, was one of the few of this wheel arrangement operated by the road. The photo is believed to have been taken in 1866. (Courtesy of Southern Pacific)

DIXIE CUT, in the timbered region near Gold Run, California, is depicted in this construction scene of early 1866. Horse-drawn dump carts are moving the excavated earth from the deep cut being hacked through the crest of the ridge by pick and shovel gangs. The locomotive appears to be Central Pacific's No. 11, the ARCTIC, a shiny 4-4-0 built by Mason in 1865 and in active service until 1892. (Courtesy of Southern Pacific)

alongside one of the huge 4-8-8-2 cab-in-front behemoths that steamed over the mountain grades of the system. Nor was this an illusion, for the *Huntington* was only about 29 feet in length, compared with the 125-foot plus stretch of the big cab-forwards. The rosters carried steam engines of practically every type and description and their colorful operation lent tones of grandeur to the Western scene.

The end of this golden era of steam railroading was quite accurately prophesied by Mr. E. McD. Johnstone in an 1888 publication closing with these words:

"As we now write over the old stage horse that lies his weary bones upon the hillside, so when steam has had its day, there shall also be written over the iron horse, as over all things mortal, THE END."

SCHENECTADY WORKS PRODUCT of 1868 vintage was this 4-6-0 named the PLUTO, assigned Central Pacific No. 59. Three sister engines were constructed by Schenectady in the same year to become Central Pacific's No. 56, the GRIZZLY, No. 57, the BISON, and No. 58, the PLACER. These wood-eating ten-wheelers boosted tonnage over the stiff Sierra grades and served faithfully for many years. (Courtesy of Southern Pacific)

MOUNTAIN TERMINAL, the Central Pacific station of Cisco nestled on the timbered western slope of the Sierra under the flank of Signal Peak, towering 7,860 feet into the blue. This rare photo shows the big station building at upper right, with covered wood sheds for the engines alongside the main line to the left of the station. The spur track at lower left led back into the flat below the depot where rows of mountain freight wagons can be seen lined up at the warehouse; a passenger train stands on this spur by the tiers of cord wood. A locomotive is headed into the two-stall roundhouse beyond the old "gallows" turntable, while in the foreground stands Engine No. 17, the IDAHO; after the road was completed, this 4-6-0 had her firebox extended in the Ogden Shops and blew up while on her second trip after the renovation, killing her crew. (Courtesy of Southern Pacific)

OLD STONE ROUNDHOUSE at Rocklin, California, provides the setting for this view of Central Pacific's No. 68, named the PEOQUOP. The 4-6-0 was built by McKay & Aldus in 1868 and later became Southern Pacific's No. 2001, scrapped in 1933. (Courtesy of David L. Joslyn)

MOUNTAIN POWER, this brass-bound 4-6-0 was Central Pacific's No. 82, the BUFFALO. Built by Rogers Locomotive Works in 1868, she had 56 inch drivers, 18 x 24 inch cylinders, and tipped the scales at 77,450 pounds. This photo shows her at Truckee, California, in 1879. (Courtesy of G. M. Best)

CENTRAL PACIFIC SHOPS at Carlin, Nevada, are shown in this photo taken about 1869. The hard usage to which the motive power was subjected during construction made frequent repairs necessary. The eight-wheeler in the center of this picture has lost her pilot, while to the right can be seen a boiler and running gear, stripped of cab and stack. (Tecrasilk photo, Grahame Hardy collection)

TRUCKEE, CALIFORNIA, in 1869. Three mountain engines of the Central Pacific stand on the track at the right, wooded, watered, and ready to do battle with the Sierra grades. Engine at left heads a string of freight cars standing under the roofed depot, a structure designed to protect operations during the heavy snowfall of winter. In later years a branch line railroad was built from Truckee up to Lake Tahoe, replacing the stage coaches and sleighs that had carried tourists up to the beautiful mountain lake. (Courtesy of Southern Pacific)

TERRIBLE WINTER OF 1868 hurled tons of snow down upon the struggling crews of the Central Pacific. Huge drifts blocked the Sierra passes, forcing nearly all phases of construction work to a halt, with the exception of some underground tunneling operations. This rare old view shows the mountain terminal of Cisco, between Emigrant Gap and Summit, with the facilities nearly buried by the white hell that choked the road. (Courtesy of Southern Pacific)

DRIFT BUSTER. As the thin ribbons of iron struggled east across the Sierra, the crews of the Central Pacific battled the heavy snowfalls of winter. Miles of snowsheds were later built, but the open sections of the road were exposed to the white blanket and the use of snow plows was mandatory. This 1868 photo from the Southern Pacific's archives shows A. W. Mc-Pherson and the Central Pacific's wedge plow No. 1. (Courtesy of Southern Pacific)

THE STORM KINGS AT WORK. Seven locomotives ram a wedge plow through the snow blocking the Central Pacific's main stem in the lofty Sierra Nevada in the years before the advent of the rotary plow. This scene was photographed in the 1870's. Hand-picked engine crews were assigned to this hazardous winter task, and fully earned their unofficial title of the "Storm Kings." Bucking snow required delicate judgment and a full cargo of cool nerve. (Courtesy of Southern Pacific)

CENTRAL PACIFIC'S NO. 118, a Danforth-built American type outshopped in 1868, was named the GREY EAGLE. She was the first C. P. locomotive assigned to fire service and carried a pump mounted on the forward section of her boiler; note the elaborate builders' plate located between her drivers. The miles of wooden snowsheds, galleries, and timber-lined tunnels were extremely vulnerable to fire started by sparks from engines struggling up the stiff grades of the Sierra. (Courtesy of Southern Pacific)

LAND OF MANY SNOWS. This 1875 picture of the Central Pacific terminal at Truckee, California, shows the roofed-over turntable and the roundhouse, with the old harp type switch lined for the turntable lead. Three locomotives, headed by Engine No. 199, stand wooded and ready to ramble. Barrels on the roofs of the wooden terminal buildings were kept filled with water for fire protection. (Courtesy of Southern Pacific)

CENTRAL PACIFIC WRECKING TRAIN of 1883 is shown here at Truckee, handled by Engine No. 26, the SAMSON. The odd 0-6-0 tank type and her sister locomotive, No. 27, the GOLIAH, were built by Danforth, Cook & Company in 1867; the GOLIAH spent most of her days switching around the old terminal at Wadsworth, Nevada, and later was used at Carlin. This photo shows the early type of hand-powered wrecking crane, equipped with manila lines and wooden blocks. The boss wrecker was a figure of local prestige on most Western roads, skilled in his ability to fish cars and locomotives out of canyons with a maze of ropes resembling a giant spider web. (Courtesy of Southern Pacific)

HOME, SWEET HOME. Central Pacific crews, laboring across the Nevada desert, lived under canvas as the rails marched east. This photo shows a typical camp at the end of track; the lines festooned with laundry are an indication that the boys have "boiled up." The camp cars, spurred out against the bleak hill, housed construction officials and their families, for many of the foremen were accompanied by wives and children as they supervised the building of the first transcontinental railway. (Courtesy of Southern Pacific)

EASY GOING. After the grueling climb over the steep and rocky Sierra passes, the crews of the Central Pacific raced across the level Nevada desert. Grading crews had prepared large sections of roadbed far in advance of the actual track laying; a force of 3,000 men with 400 horses and carts had graded through Palisade Canyon while the end of track was 300 miles to the rear. Water was often scarce and at one point the drinking supply for men and horses had to be hauled for forty miles. (Courtesy of Southern Pacific)

CAMP VICTORY, UTAH. On April 28th, 1869, eight brawny Irishmen muscled more than 3,500 rails, over 1,000 tons of iron, into position to set a Central Pacific track laying record of slightly over 10 miles. This photo, taken the day the record was established, shows the work trains and outfit cars at the railhead called Camp Victory, later Rozel station, near Promontory, Utah. The bearded gent in the dark suit, standing on the flat car, is James H. Strowbridge, Construction Superintendent for the Central Pacific; a profane man with the reputation of being a "driver," Strowbridge was well chosen for the difficult task of pushing the rails east to meet the rival Union Pacific forces. (Courtesy of Southern Pacific)

IRON HORSE. A family of Indians gather on the Nevada plains to examine the CHAMPION, Central Pacific's Engine 50. The track, innocent of ballast and with unevenly spaced ties, suggests that this photo was taken shortly after the rails were spiked home on this section. Note the ornate bell bracket, drum-shaped oil headlight, and fancy builder's plate mounted between the drivers of this McKay & Aldus eight-wheeler of 1867. (Courtesy of Southern Pacific)

THE JARRETT & PALMER SPECIAL made headline news in 1876. On June 1st of that year, theatrical producers Jarrett and Palmer climbed aboard a chartered train, along with their excursion party, and departed from New York at 12:40 A.M. In the record time of 84 hours, 17 minutes, including the ferry ride, the group arrived at the Market Street terminal in San Francisco. A single Central Pacific locomotive, No. 149, the BLACK FOX, handled the special from Ogden to Oakland in 23 hours, 45 minutes. Her crews included Engineers H. S. "Hank" Small and James Wright, and three firemen, W. C. Dean, J. W. Brown, and Martin Duxstad. These hardys, together with Road Foreman of Engines Ben Smith, are posed here with the Schenectady speed queen, built in 1868. (Courtesy of David L. Joslyn)

WINNEMUCCA STATION of the Central Pacific as it appeared about 1869. The funnel stacker at right is coupled to one of the numerous water cars required for operation in the arid regions. Location of early terminals was often decided by the availability of a satisfactory water supply. Note the rough and crooked alignment of the rails on the track in the foreground (Tecrasilk photo, Grahame Hardy collection)

SADDLE-TANK SHUNTER, the Central Pacific's No. 32 bore the name AJAX; her sister engine, No. 33, was named the ACHILLES. Both locomotives, the first 0-6-0 types on the road, were built by the New Jersey Locomotive Company in 1867. The Central Pacific later converted them to 4-4-0's. (Courtesy of Southern Pacific)

QUEEN OF THE HUMBOLDT, this beautiful American type posed for her portrait out on the desert around 1879, ably assisted by her engine crew. Built by Schenectady in 1869, she was Central Pacific's No. 158, named the EUREKA. Note the high gloss on her polished jacket and the six-wheel tank trucks. Her tender is piled high with the coal that replaced the wood of earlier days as fuel for the Central's motive power. This engine later became Southern Pacific's No. 1225 and was scrapped in 1901. (Courtesy of Southern Pacific)

DESERT FREIGHT CREW posed for this photograph at Mill City, Nevada, in 1884. The pretty diamond stack 4-4-0 is Central Pacific's No. 159, the DIANA. She was turned out by Schenectady in 1869, Shop No. 559 and had 60 inch drivers, 16x24 inch cylinders, and weighed 65,500 pounds. The engine later became Southern Pacific's 1226 and was scrapped in 1899. Note the fancy headlight brackets and the figure of the eagle perched atop her sand dome. (Courtesy of David L. Joslyn).

IN UNITY THERE IS STRENGTH. A pair of husky Central Pacific 4-6-0's, tanks piled high with wood, join couplers to hoist a freight drag over the steep grades that confronted eastbound traffic climbing out of the California flatlands. Leading engine is No. 68, the PEOQUOP, built by McKay & Aldus in 1867. (Courtesy of Southern Pacific)

EL GOBERNADOR, Spanish for THE GOVERNOR, was built under the supervision of General Master Mechanic A. J. Stevens in the Central Pacific's Sacramento Shops in 1883. Her first valve gear, using rotary valves, proved to be impractical and was replaced with a gear designed by Stevens. The giant 4-10-0, weighing 146,-000 pounds, had 21x36 inch cylinders and 57 inch drivers. She was assigned road number 237 and placed in service in March, 1884. Sent down to Bakersfield in partly dismantled condition, she was reassembled for helper service over the Tehachapi grade, but proved unsatisfactory, her boiler being unable to furnish sufficient steam. The engine was dismantled at Sacramento in 1894, her boiler going into service as a stationary for the machine shops. This rare photo shows EL GOBERNADOR in service at Tehachapi in 1885. (Courtesy of Southern Pacific)

MOVING WEST, immigrant cars are coupled in the rear of this Central Pacific freight train at Mill City, Nevada, in 1883; the station is located between Imlay and Winnemucca. Crew, left to right, include Brakeman Ed Doolittle, Conductor Ike Cross, Engineer George Abbey, Fireman Johnny Goldie, and Brakeman Tom Hogan. The English setter on the pilot beam is typical of the mascot dogs that rode in Western engine cabs in the days before rules hedged in the crews and ended much of the colorful individuality of the operating personnel. (Courtesy of Southern Pacific)

STURDY TENWHEELER, this engine was the second Central Pacific locomotive to bear road number 19. She was built in the road's Sacramento Shops around 1886 and was equipped with A. J. Stevens' "monkey motion" valve gear. In addition to this valve gear, Stevens designed a "boiler economizer", an early feedwater heating device, and many of the locomotives built under his supervision were fitted with radial staybolts of his design applied to their boilers. (Courtesy of Southern Pacific)

TANDEM TEAKETTLES, these Central Pacific 4-4-0's point up what is reported to be the first fruit train to leave California. The leading engine, No. 183, sports the fluted domes and brass acorns that mark her as a Rogers product; she rolled out of the New Jersey plant in 1872. This pioneer fruit block paved the way for untold millions of tons of perishables that have since rambled out of California on their way to Eastern markets. (Courtesy of Southern Pacific)

DESERT PRINCESS, this beautiful 4-4-0 is the No. 1 of the Southern Pacific Railroad of Arizona, shown here posing with a bunch of the boys against the sandy slopes at Yuma in 1881. Built by Schenectady in 1879, she later became Southern Pacific's No. 81, then No. 1312 before she was cut up in 1918. Note the canteen hanging on the tender at the gangway; the problem of water supply was often acute in the arid stretches of Indian-infested desert. (Courtesy of G. M. Best)

COLORADO CROSSING. This view, taken in 1877, shows a Southern Pacific locomotive on the bridge spanning the Colorado River at Yuma, Arizona. The rails arrived on the California shore in May, 1877, but there was delay in obtaining permission to cross onto the Yuma Indian Reservation and the wooden truss structure, including a draw span for steamboat traffic, was not completed until September 30th of that year. On the low mesa in the background can be seen the buildings of Fort Yuma, historic old Army post. (Courtesy Southern Pacific)

RARE OLD PHOTO shows three Central Pacific locomotives coupled behind a snowplow at Cisco, California, during the hard winter of 1867. The deep drifts of snow heaped along the track illustrate the winter storm conditions confronting the iron men and their woodburning locomotives in their battle to keep the railroad open. (Courtesy of Southern Pacific)

POLISHED BEAUTY, this shiny 4-4-0 is Southern Pacific's Engine 24, shown here at the head end of a passenger train at Los Angeles, California, in 1882. The diamond stacker was constructed by Schenectady in 1875, bearing Shop No. 980, and sported 63 inch drivers and 16x24 inch cylinders. Later renumbered 1233, she was scrapped in 1902. Note the large image of the eagle on the lens of the big oil headlight. (Courtesy of G. M. Best collection)

CENTRAL PACIFIC SHOPS in Sacramento constructed No. 187 in 1873, one year after they had turned out their first engine. The shops turned out a number of fine locomotives under the direction of Andrew J. Stevens, who was appointed General Master Mechanic in 1869 and served until his death in 1888. The engine shown here later became Southern Pacific's No. 1367. (Courtesy of Southern Pacific)

NEAT AS A PIN, this clearly detailed photograph shows Engine No. 7 of the Southern Pacific as she appeared about 1875. Originally No. 7 of the San Francisco & San Jose Railroad and named the ATLANTIC, she was the second locomotive built by H. J. Booth & Company of San Francisco, erected in 1865. She later became Southern Pacific's No. 1231 and was scrapped in 1895. The San Francisco & San Jose was taken over by the Espee shortly after completion to San Jose and served as a link in the extension south to Los Angeles. (Courtesy of G. M. Best)

DIAMOND STACK IN DOWNTOWN 'FRISCO. This photograph taken in 1887 shows the first Southern Pacific General Office at 4th and Townsend Streets in San Francisco. The 3-story structure was occupied in 1872 when the original offices were removed from 54 K Street in Sacramento; the fourth floor was added in 1877. A wisp of smoke curls from the brass-bound eight-wheeler at the right while pedestrians hurry on their appointed ways. Note the old semaphore signal on the pole above the horsecar; the lettering on the upper panels of the vehicle drawn by the two oat-burners reads, "Fourth, Kearny & North Beach." (Courtesy of Southern Pacific)

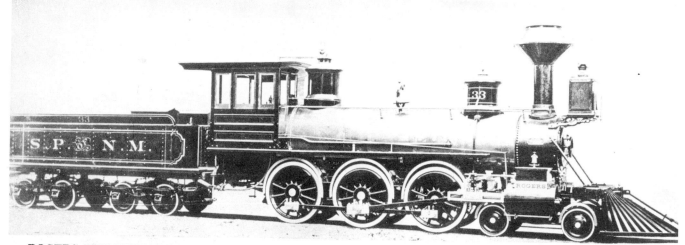

ROGERS TEN-WHEELER, No. 33 bears the lettering of the Southern Pacific of New Mexico, a railroad incorporated in 1879 to build east across New Mexico Territory. The road was completed into El Paso in 1881 and was absorbed into the Southern Pacific in 1885. The locomotive was renumbered several times, ending her days as Southern Pacific's No. 2109, scrapped in 1931.

CHINESE TEA CARRIER replaced the traditional water boy serving the gangs of coolie labor employed during construction of the Central Pacific. This "tea boy" is shown posed against a rugged backdrop of Sierra grade near the portal of a tunnel. When Charles Crocker was criticized for using Oriental labor on Central Pacific masonry work, he reminded the critics that the departed ancestors of his "pets" had built the Great Wall of China. (Courtesy of Southern Pacific)

GREAT SALT LAKE TRESTLE was completed on October 26th, 1903, when the final pile in the 12-mile trestle was thumped home. The new Lucin cut-off carried Southern Pacific trains across the northern portion of Great Salt Lake, leaving the historic meeting point at Promontory off the main line on the old original route around the northern shores of the lake. The old route continued in service as a branch until 1942, when it was abandoned and the rails torn up. (Courtesy of Southern Pacific)

SOUTHERN PACIFIC OF NEW MEXICO'S No. 19 was one of a series of 4-4-0's built for that road by Schenectady in 1881-82. This engine had 60 inch drivers, 17x24 inch cylinders, and weighed 73,700 pounds. She later became Southern Pacific's No. 178, was renumbered 1349, and was scrapped in 1900. Engineer Tom Martin stands in the gangway in this early photo. (Courtesy of Southern Pacific.)

WESTWARD HO! The locomotive BLACK HAWK headed the first Union Pacific construction train into Ogden on March 8th, 1869. Built by Hinkley & Williams of Boston in 1861, the three-domed American Standard weighed 31 tons and had 15 x 24 inch cylinders. In May, 1869, the Union Pacific turned this engine over to Brigham Young to become No. 1 of the Utah Central Railroad. She is shown here in service between Ogden and Salt Lake; the photograph was taken by Engineer C. F. Husbands in 1876. (Courtesy of Central Company, Daughters of Utah Pioneers)

Rails West.

The legends and stories relating to the construction of the Union Pacific's portion of the first transcontinental railroad have often been told, but the aura of thrilling adventure never grows dim. The ribbons of iron left the civilized and settled region along the Missouri River and headed westerly into the setting sun. Before the railroad builders lay a vast distance of plain, desert, and mountain. Much of the route ran through virgin country, inhabited only by wild animals and even wilder savages. Truly, the task of building and operating a railroad through this forbidding area was a monumental one.

It is not the purpose of this work to go into the complex problems concerning the financing of the Union Pacific. The promoters and investors were often pressed for money to prevent the work from

HEADING FOR THE FRONT, a load of covered wagons rolls along behind a Union Pacific locomotive approaching a water tank on the arid western plains. The wagons were probably a part of the railroad's supply train system. The bearded gent on the wagon seat flourishes a revolver, a reminder that the Union Pacific crews were frequently menaced by Indians who resented the invasion of their tribal haunts and hunting grounds. (Tecrasilk Photo, Grahame Hardy Collection)

UNION PACIFIC TIE TRAIN, handled by Engine 22, a 4-4-0, pauses in a cut during construction days. The ties are cut from small trees and hewed flat on top and bottom; the sides are left in their natural state. This photograph, taken about 1868, shows the outside wooden brake beam and the link and pin coupler on the tender of the locomotive. (Tecrasilk Photo, Grahame Hardy Collection)

halting, and some rather devious methods of financial dealings ended in the Credit Mobilier scandal.

Ground for the Union Pacific was broken at Omaha, Nebraska, on December 2nd, 1863, but there was a controversy over the route and the first 40 miles of line were not graded until the end of 1865. Track laying had been commenced in July of 1865, but it was not until the following year that construction work got under way in earnest. Peter A. Dey, the road's first Chief Engineer, resigned because he disapproved the construction contracts. Dey was succeeded by Grenville M. Dodge, a Massachusetts man who was experienced in Western engineering and railroad work. Dodge had risen to the rank of Major General in the Union Army during the Civil War, was seriously wounded twice, and later placed in command of the troops engaged in fighting the Indians in the West. While active in the Indian campaigns, Dodge discovered the pass later used by the Union Pacific. Returning from a campaign in the Yellowstone region in 1865, Dodge and his troopers had a brisk brush with the Indians in the area between Crow Creek and Lone Tree Creek, but in the action of the running skirmish he located the feasible railway route, naming the place Sherman Hill, in honor of his old Army commander, Gen. William T. Sherman.

The route of the Union Pacific was bought and paid for with the lifeblood of brave men. One of the first to fall in battle was L. L. Hills, chief of a survey party locating the line at the east base of the Rockies in the spring of 1867. The Hills survey crew was jumped by Indians about 6 miles east of Cheyenne and Hills was killed. A young axman, J. M. Eddy, rallied the party after the death of the leader and brought them to the safety of the Army post at Camp Collins. In July of 1867 the braves of the Sioux nation swooped down on a surveyors' camp located on Rock Creek, surprising a wood-gathering detail led by a young man named Clark, a nephew of Thurlow Reed, prominent New Yorker. Clark and a member of his escort were killed and several others in the party were wounded.

Percy T. Brown, chief of the survey party attacked at the Rock Creek camp, was jumped by a war party of 30 Sioux while engaged in running a line across the Laramie Plains. Brown and his escort party of 8 troopers were engaged by the warriors about noon and took up a defensive position on a little knoll, where they stood off their beseigers until nearly dark, but in the last brief charge before darkness fell, Brown received a severe abdominal wound. As

THE GANDY DANCERS. Near Devil's Gate, Utah, a Union Pacific track gang levels a section of track, using a pry pole, shovels, and lining bars. Many of the track men during construction through this region were Mormons; Union Pacific construction gangs included a large percentage of Irishmen, many of them veterans of the Civil War. Though the work was hard and the pay low, the section gangs were the buckos who kept the tracks in shape for the safe and swift passage of the trains. Toiling unsheltered from the elements, they left their own monuments in the shining ribbons of silver that crosshatch the Pacific West. (Courtesy of Union Pacific Railroad)

THE SINGING WIRES. A crew of linemen string the first telegraph alongside the Union Pacific tracks in Utah's Weber Canyon. As the rails marched west, the line crews kept pace with their poles and wire, bringing the strident chatter of key and sounder into the isolated regions of the vanishing frontier. The small crews of linemen were vulnerable to Indian attacks, but the danger was lessened when the road reached Utah, the Mormons having maintained amicable relations with the native tribesmen. (Courtesy of Union Pacific Railroad)

RED RAIDERS' VICTIM, the No. 53 of the Union Pacific was derailed by Indians near Plum Creek, Nebraska, in August of 1867. Engineer "Bully" Brooks and his fireman were both killed and the wrecked train plundered by the savages before a rescue party arrived. The American Standard is shown here equipped with fire-fighting apparatus; note the footboard extending along the side of the tender. When not in use, the fire hose was carried on the reel mounted on the cab roof. (Courtesy of Union Pacific Historical Museum)

soon as the Sioux captured the horses of the survey party they departed, and the little group set out afoot through the tall growth of sage. The injured Brown pleaded with his escort to leave him and save their own skins, but the troopers were made of the stuff that stands. They fabricated a litter, using their carbines for supports, and carried the wounded man some 15 miles to the La Clede Stage Station, but their efforts were in vain and Brown died shortly after they reached the station with him.

Not only did the Indians war on the surveying parties and burn the isolated telegraph stations, but they also raided the grading and track crews, frequently driving off the stock used by these crews. To combat these depredations, the construction crews were regularly drilled in military tactics and went to their work fully armed, ready to swap pick or spike maul for carbine at an instant's notice.

Even after operations of the road commenced, the danger from Indians was not wholly abated and the train and engine crews were attacked in several instances. The capture of a train near Plum Creek, the killing of the crew, and the looting of the wreckage is one of the more publicized instances of the dangers from this quarter to which the operating personnel were exposed.

The locomotives in use by the Union Pacific during the construction period were about the same as those used on the Central Pacific. The first motive power was boated up the muddy Missouri to the Omaha landing to be placed in service, and river steamboats were used to transport rail, machinery, and other supplies to the road's eastern terminus.

Wood was used for fuel in the engines, and in this regard the Central Pacific had a decided advantage. The Sierra slopes were thickly clad with dense forests of pitchy fir and pine, while the shallow Nebraska watercourses boasted but a thin fringe of cottonwood. This was a poor type of wood for engine fuel, and equally poor for use as tie material, being so soft that it would not hold the spikes properly. Cottonwood ties were treated by a process known as "Burnetizing," the ties being placed in a metal cylinder from which the air was exhausted, then a solution of chloride of zinc forced into the porous wood under pressure. Tie hackers went up the Missouri River in search of timber suitable for railroad use, the ties being rafted downstream to the terminus.

As the rails extended west, ties were chopped in the sparse forests of the Elk and the Medicine Bow mountains and tie drives came floating down the Medicine Bow, North Platte, and Laramie rivers. Pine ties were driven down Henry's Fork and the waters of the Bear River and the Weber for use on the western end of the road.

The majority of construction on the Union Pacific was done by the firm of J. S. & D. T. Casement, brothers who contracted for the track laying and much of the grading. John Stephen Casement was a colorful character, born on the Isle of Man, and a man with considerable railroad experience. He served in the Union Army during the Civil War, rising to the rank of a breveted brigadier general.

With his brother, Dan Casement, he organized his construction forces in a well-equipped and disciplined manner. After the Civil War ended, many soldiers drifted west to seek employment on the railroad and it was from this trained element that "Jack" Casement built his fighting, hard-working crew. The gangs included large numbers of Irishmen, and the drinking and fighting that took place around the camps at the end of track is legendary. Equally as notorious was "Hell On Wheels," a portable collection of saloons, bagnios, and gambling dens that followed the brawling gangs from railhead to railhead. In several instances, the railroad and

CLIMBING THE WASATCH, the Union Pacific built a great switchback near the head of Echo Canyon, Utah, in 1868 as a temporary expedient to handle construction traffic until a tunnel could be driven through the ridge at the summit. This rare view shows a side-tank locomotive standing on the old switchback line beneath a bridge on the relocated grade. The 4-4-0 above heads a work train engaged in completing the fill at the left. This switchback operation was abandoned in the first week of June, 1869. (Courtesy of Union Pacific Historical Museum)

construction officials took over and cleaned up the wildest of the towns along the road, one notable instance being the subduing of tough elements infesting Julesburg.

Building across the vast prairie lands had other advantages in addition to easy grading. At the time the Union Pacific was thrusting iron rails and brass-bound locomotives across the plains, vast herds of shaggy buffalo were still roaming the region. The contractors hired meat hunters to kill these huge beasts, thus assuring themselves of a steady supply of fresh meat for the camp messes. Elk, deer, and antelope also fell before the rifles of the camp hunters. The buffalo could be a nuisance as well as a roaming commissary. The animals migrated in such numbers that the herds occasionally blocked the tracks, halting trains until they had passed on their way. The telegraph poles furnished convenient scratching material, and the shedding bulls often rubbed against them until they toppled, bringing the wire to earth and disrupting rail communications.

Floods plagued the road during construction, a severe storm in March of 1867 sweeping away a great deal of the grade through the valley of the Platte and in some instances washing away rails, ties, and bridges. The road also had troubles with snow in the severe winters, the drifts filling up cuts and stalling trains. Much of this trouble was later overcome by raising the grade slightly and by constructing snow fences that held the drifts clear of the track.

As the end of track marched west, the Union Pacific established terminals and roundhouses to handle the switching and care for the motive power. The names of these places had a splash of color that made the Old West so enchanting to the folks "back East" . . . Grand Island, North Platte, Cheyenne, Sherman, Laramie, Medicine Bow, Rawlins, Green River, and that home of the proverbial badman, Bitter Creek.

Water supply was a problem in the arid stretches of the Great Plains, and the road used windmills as well as steam pumping plants to furnish the necessary water for locomotives and terminal use. Since nearly all construction material had to be brought out to the end of track from Omaha, including timbers for bridge building, the light iron rail used soon began to wear out, and a rerolling mill was set up at Laramie to recondition the worn wrought iron.

Much of the grading done in Utah, after the road had topped the Continental Divide and driven across Wyoming, was the work of local residents. The Latter-day Saints desired to help the railroad reach the Salt Lake Valley, in addition to gathering in the gold coin being dispensed for construction work. A number of Mormons took contracts and these included some of the heaviest rock work encountered on the entire route. The longest tunnel on the Union Pacific, No. 2, was located at the head of Utah's Echo Canyon and was over 770 feet long. The rock formation within the bore was so soft that it crumbled badly and the tunnel had to be lined with timbering. The Union Pacific was pushing construction as rapidly as possible in the race against the Central Pacific, so a temporary line that re-

UNION PACIFIC'S MAIN LINE in Utah is shown in this magnificent view, with a Rogers eight-wheeler passing through the truss bridge over the Weber River. Piercing the rocky barrier in the background is the east portal of Tunnel No. 3. The Union Pacific had comparatively few tunnels to dig, while the rival Central Pacific crews had to drill bore after bore to conquer the Sierra Nevada. (Courtesy of Union Pacific Historical Museum)

PHOTOGRAPHER'S SPECIAL on the Union Pacific during construction of the road was handled by this odd 4-4-0 sporting side tanks and footboards. A huge set of elk antlers adorn the roof of the car fitted up especially for use of the travelling camera artist. Note the ornate bell and headlight brackets. (Courtesy of Union Pacific Historical Museum)

WASATCH METROPOLIS, this is Echo City, Utah, shortly after the advent of the Union Pacific. Several frame buildings are scattered along the rail yards located in the bowl of this pleasant mountain-hemmed valley. The tents in the foreground house business establishments, masquerading behind wooden false fronts. (Courtesy of Union Pacific Railroad)

portedly included a switchback was built around the site of Tunnel No. 2 and this was still in use when the rails met at Promontory on May 10th, 1869. At Tunnel No. 3, in Weber Canyon, another temporary track was laid around the jutting spur of rock to permit construction trains to advance while the tunnel was still unfinished.

The Union Pacific rails reached Ogden on March 3rd, 1869, and the town later became an important terminal point. The road crossed the Weber River on a span erected at 24th Street and a permanent depot was built in the fall of 1869. Located about one-half block west of Wall Avenue, between 24th and 25th streets, the one story structure was composed of boards set perpendicular and was painted red. The depot was about 40 feet long and housed the offices, station master, and baggage room. Daniel Gamble was the first telegraph operator in the Ogden office and 90 years later, his grandson and namesake, Daniel L. Gamble, still carries on the railroad tradition, being employed as an engineman on the Southern Pacific's Portland Division. Ogden's first station master was W. N. Cleveland and the first ticket agent was William Horsefall. The Union Pacific built a roundhouse on the west side of Wall Avenue in Ogden in the fall of 1870. This structure, containing four stalls, stood slightly north of 24th Street.

West of Ogden, the line swung north across the Bear River flats to the freighting metropolis of Corinne. The first engine rumbled over the Bear River

bridge and entered Corinne with a string of flat cars on April 7th, 1869. The booming rail town became noted for its Opera House, dedicated on July 4th, 1870. The main floor, used for dancing, was set on springs of the type used on railroad cars and was a famed attraction. This Opera House was the scene of many productions by the leading stock companies of the nation, most of them playing a one-night stand here while en route across the continent.

The story of the meeting of the rails at Promontory has been told in the preceding chapter, thus drawing to a close the account of the construction of the first rail line to link the Atlantic with the Pacific.

Through passenger service was established soon after the two roads met, and the first notable excursion from coast to coast was that of the Boston Board of Trade, travelling from Boston to San Francisco and return in the early summer of 1870. The special consisted of 8 cars and carried 129 passengers; in the baggage car was a printing press that turned out the *"Trans-continental,"* probably the first newspaper ever published upon a moving railway train.

The Union Pacific trains handled other cargo in addition to Back Bay tourists and emigrants riding in bare wooden coaches, however, and this traffic was to cause the road no little trouble. The mines of the West were spilling out their treasures and the Union Pacific express cars hauled specie and bullion worth untold fortunes. The shady gentry who had preyed on the treasure boxes carried aboard stage coaches were not long in tapping this golden flow of riches.

On September 18th, 1877, a Union Pacific train rolled up to the water tank at Big Springs, Nebraska. Masked men confronted the startled crew and entered the express car in charge of Expressman Charley Miller. The gang consisted of six tough hombres, led by Sam Bass and Joe Collins. These bold highwaymen made off with about $60,000 in freshly-minted twenty dollar gold pieces, plus an estimated $1,000 worth of money, jewels, and watches plundered from the train's passengers.

This appropriation of "easy money" was to prove contagious, and the art of train robbery rapidly increased. Out in Wyoming, the notorious Hole-in-the-Wall Gang tried their luck with the first section of the Overland Express early in June, 1899. Near Wilcox station, Engineer W. R. Jones was flagged by a red lantern, but the flagmen turned out to be outlaws who roughed up the runner considerably for his lack of cooperation. They blew up the express car and relieved Expressman Woodcock of an estimated $30,000 in cash and negotiable bonds, then rode off into the wastelands.

At 8:00 P. M. on the night of August 29th, 1900, they repeated this caper, stopping Union Pacific's Train No. 3 in the vicinity of Table Rock, near Tipton, Wyoming. They captured Conductor E. J. Kerrigan and forced him to accompany them to the express car, where, by coincidence, they again encountered Expressman Woodcock. At first he refused to open the car, but the bandits readied explosives to blast him out and Conductor Kerrigan convinced him that nothing could be gained by sacrificing his life. With the car open, the robbers blew open the safe and rode away with a take estimated at over $5,000. The Union Pacific, weary of these repeated hold-ups, rigged up a special train, complete with a baggage car fitted out with a ramp for unloading horses. This car carried the mounts for six picked posse members and the instructions went out to these manhunters to bring the robbers in, dead or alive, the next time they held up a Union Pacific train. A locomotive with a picked crew was kept ready to roll, day or night, to the scene of the next robbery. The "Wild Bunch," led by notorious Butch Cassidy, heard of these precautions and left the country. Several members of the gang were to come to violent ends, but not until they had robbed a train on the Great Northern near Malta, Montana, on the afternoon of July 3rd, 1901. Two of the leaders of this gang were Robert Parker, better

DINNER STOP. This photo shows the WHAT CHEER DINING HALL, a typical eating house along the main stem of the Union Pacific in 1870. This wooden frame structure stood alongside the tracks of the Overland Route at Wasatch, Utah. Note the baby carriage with the 3-wheeled running gear and the gong held by the man in the right foreground. This gong was used to summon hungry passengers to meals when a train halted in the days before dining cars came into use. (Courtesy of Union Pacific Railroad)

NATURAL SCENIC WONDERS along the Union Pacific were not as plentiful as those encountered farther west, where the deep canyons and snow-capped peaks lined the Sierra route of the Central Pacific. However, unusual rock formations created attractions for Union Pacific crews and passengers, especially in the canyons of northeastern Utah. This 4-4-0 and her two-car train are arrayed in front of the famous Pulpit Rock, located in Utah's Echo Canyon. The picture, taken in the 1870's, shows the light rail supported by hand-hewn cross-ties. (Courtesy of Union Pacific Railroad)

known by his alias, "Butch Cassidy," and Harry Longbaugh, the "Sundance Kid." Both are reputed to have fled to South America, where they were gunned down after a series of daring robberies.

After the completion of the transcontinental road, the Union Pacific began to branch out in the region west of the Rockies This expansion was fostered through the mediums of the Oregon Short Line and other railroad companies.

The Oregon Short Line construction project left the old main track at Granger, Wyoming, and built northwesterly from that junction point; construction started in 1881 and the end of track crossed the Idaho line at a point near Montpelier on June 16th, 1882. The problems faced by the contractors on the Short Line were considerably different from those confronting the original builders of the Union Pacific. The Indian and the buffalo were on the wane, but the tough element was still populating the western region in increasing numbers. Shoshone, Idaho, had the deserved reputation of being one of roughest towns in the west during the 1880's, and the payrolls for the grading crews working in the vicinity were constantly threatened by gangs of armed badmen.

The grading was mostly of a very difficult nature, the Wood River country section of the Oregon Shrot Line running across ancient lava beds. Con-

ditions improved when the road neared Boise, the lava flows giving way to soil that was more readily moved by teams and scrapers. From McCammon to Pocatello, the Oregon Short Line used the narrow gauge tracks of the existing Utah & Northern. The standard gauge cars were raised by a device and their trucks rolled out from under them. A set of narrow gauge trucks was then wheeled into place, the car lowered, and moved off on the narrow gauge line. In the late 1880's, the old Utah & Northern, under Union Pacific control, was widened to standard gauge. The 262 mile section between Pocatello, Idaho, and Garrison, Montana, was all changed on one day, July 24th, 1887. Work of shifting the rail out to standard gauge was begun early in the morning, with every available man pressed into service. By mid-afternoon the job was complete and this section of slim gauge was only a memory. The Utah & Northern route from McCammon to Ogden was changed to standard gauge in 1889-90, the old original route being altered and shortened.

When the Oregon Short Line made connections with the Oregon Railway & Navigation Company at Huntington, Oregon, the junction made it possible for the Union Pacific to serve as a link between Portland and the cities of the eastern regions. The first through passenger service began operations on January 1st, 1885. In later years, the Union Pacific acquired complete control of the two roads, bringing their western terminus down to a Pacific Coast seaport.

Life on the western end of this new route was also far from dull. The line crossed the rugged Blue Mountains on a steep and crooked grade where one engineer achieved lasting fame. A train dispatcher had let a passenger train out of Kamela with a lap order in their possession, headed for almost certain destruction in a head-on collision with an opposing train; there was no open telegraph station between the two trains and no block signals to stop them. "Hair Oil Pete" St. Cyr, a veteran mountain runner, gave chase with a low-wheeled freight engine, caught up with the passenger train, and whistled them down before the opposing train was met; his freight engine, designed for slow speed, was ruined in the race against death. St. Cyr's unusual monicker was bestowed because he allegedly greased his hair with valve oil from the tallowpot, a product normally used solely for locomotive lubrication.

On down in the valley of the Columbia, the call boy rounded up Engineer "Smoky" McCune at Umatilla one day for a westbound trip on freight to The Dalles. When he arrived at the enginehouse, McCune looked over his diamond-stacked eight-wheeler and then hunted up the roundhouse foreman, demanding that his engine be supplied with additional coal. The foreman refused, claiming that the engine had ample fuel for the trip. McCune left town in a huff, vowing that they would run out of coal before they reached The Dalles. He pounded the engine for all she was worth but when they reached Biggs it was apparent that the foreman had been correct and that the coal would carry them to The Dalles, but the foreman had not reckoned on "Smoky." McCune eased his engine to a halt on the Deschutes River bridge and he and the sweating fireman shoveled the remaining coal into the swift water below. The engine died a few miles beyond the bridge and had to be towed in. The Super had "Smoky" on the carpet for an investigation, but the facts were never developed. When the session ended, J. P. O'Brien, the brass hat conducting the affair, turned to McCune and said, "Smoky, you are lying to me but I can't prove it," to which McCune replied, "I know damned well you can't!"

Going east from The Dalles over this same stretch of track in the 1890's, Engineer McCune and his fireman, M. M. Sayre, hit a sand drift and turned their locomotive over. When the dust had settled, 43 of the cracker-box freight cars then in use were in the ditch, but neither McCune nor Sayre received a scratch.

Other crews on the O. R. & N. were not so fortunate. In the late 1890's, Train No. 6 hit a boulder that had fallen onto the track near Rooster Rock, between The Dalles and Portland. Engineer Bob Hunter and Fireman Miler were both killed, and a double funeral was held in Albina for these two popular enginemen.

During the wheat rush in 1901, Master Mechanic J. F. Graham was forced to doublehead the heavy drags headed east, and he conceived the idea of running sets of two engines coupled tank to tank, to avoid the necessity for turning the power at either end of the district. Engineers Hasslam and Reese caught one of these jobs and while boring along a short distance east of The Dalles, they plowed into a dune of drifted blow-sand. The freight went into the ditch, killing the crews of both engines.

In the roaring '90's, wrecks were frequent along the O. R. & N. rails through the Columbia Gorge. Engineer Ben Wilkes was seriously injured in one of these, and Engineer Bill Milligan was killed when he rode his engine into the river in a derailment east of The Dalles. Fireman M. M. Sayre narrowly escaped death by being held off his freight run for a trip on passenger. His regular engineer, Charley Johnson, and the relief fireman were both killed when Engine 444 plowed into a sand drift.

Conditions on the road were rough, but the operating men were usually equal to them. Engineers were required to repair their engines when they broke down on the road, each locomotive being

EARLY DAYS ON THE "PEDRO." Engine 56, a 4-6-0 of the San Pedro, Los Angeles & Salt Lake, carries a water car behind her tank in this photo taken at Milford, Utah, in 1901. Her crew includes Conductor Hawkins, Engineer George Brown, Fireman Bachman, and Brakemen Jackson and Johnson. The "Pedro" provided a southern route from the Salt Lake valley to the Pacific, crossing the desert regions of Utah, Nevada, and California. (Courtesy of Union Pacific Historical Museum)

THE TIDE OF EMPIRE, flowing west behind the grading gangs of the Union Pacific, halts long enough to pose for a photo on Devil's Gate Bridge in Utah. The work train is being handled by No. 117, a polished 4-4-0 with fluted sand dome hinting at her Rogers ancestry. The heaviest rock work on the Union Pacific was located in this region, and the mountain streams slowed construction by requiring costly bridging, but the cool waters were a welcome relief to the workers after the long haul across the arid plains and desert. (Courtesy of Union Pacific Railroad)

supplied with a large tool box to care for these breakdowns. Not long after the turn of the century, Arthur M. Sayre, now a retired engineer, was firing for a runner when their engine broke down, stripping herself badly. The day was a real scorcher with the heat waves shimmering on the rock ballast. The engineer surveyed the damage, cursed roundly, and sent Art up onto the tank to throw down the tool box. When this had been accomplished, the hogger called Art to assist him and they lugged the box

FREIGHT CREW of the early days poses with Union Pacific's Engine No. 12, a prototype of the power that wheeled the flood-tide of civilization into the great American West. This early photograph was probably taken in the yards at Ogden, Utah. (Courtesy of Utah State Historical Society)

down the bank and heaved it into the swift waters of the Columbia. The engineer then notified the mechanical department that his engine was broke down and that he had no tools, the tool box having been "lost" en route. The crew relaxed in the shade until the machinists from the terminal arrived to make the necessary repairs.

The lines of the old O. R. & N. were the training grounds for many capable railroaders, some of whom were destined to sit in high places. One of these was James William Corbett, the son of a railroad man, who started work as a call boy at La Grande in 1911. He became a telegrapher, then was promoted to train dispatcher, later becoming a trainmaster. Mr. Corbett's next step was to the position of superintendent, and today he holds the post of General Manager of the far-flung lines of the great Southern Pacific system.

The medium of television has made a household word of the name of Wyatt Earp, the famous Western lawman noted for his cool courage and accurate use of his Buntline special. Few, however, know that Earp had a hand in building the original Union Pacific main line. In 1865, while still in his teens, Wyatt Earp made a few trips driving one of General

Banning's six-horse coaches on the run between San Bernardino and Los Angeles, then assumed a more risky job of driving a freight team between San Pedro, California, and Prescott, Arizona, for Frank Binkley. Early in 1866, Earp left this job to skin a sixteen-horse freight outfit from San Bernardino to Salt Lake City for the noted freighter, Chris Taylor. In the spring of 1867 he left Taylor to freight for Charley Chrisman, a venture that led to his railroad work. Chrisman had taken a grading contract on the Union Pacific and Earp went to work on this job early in 1868, driving a four-horse hitch on a breaking plow that furrowed the prairie sod ahead of the grading gang. Young Wyatt Earp, then 20 years of age, soon purchased teams of his own, continuing on the Chrisman contract until the fall of 1868 when he sold his stock and departed for other adventures that were to make him famous. His last work on the Union Pacific grade was between Hams Fork and Fort Bridger, Wyoming.

Untold numbers of flanged wheels have rolled over Union Pacific rails since the woodburning engines hooted at the herds of shaggy, lumbering buffalo and engine crews kept a sharp lookout for the dust raised by Sioux war parties. The road developed its own coal mines, providing a new fuel to replace the ocstly wood, and bigger, more powerful locomotives came to shower cinders on Sherman Hill.

Today, the roar of turbines echo in the canyon of the Weber where, in the tumult of yesteryear, Mormon grading gangs hacked with pick and shovel and the rocky gorge reverbrated with the booming

UTAH TERMINAL. This was the first Union Pacific roundhouse at Echo, Utah. It was a wooden frame structure with four stalls, metal smoke-jacks, and louvered cupolas on the shingled roof. The locomotives, posed with their crews in front of the building, are, left to right, No.'s 987, 1001, 949, and 1011. All are equipped with oil headlights, link and pin couplers, wooden stave pilots, and diamond stacks.

of black powder charges. Sleek streamliners polish the Union Pacific rails in Oregon where once in the spring of 1894 the marchers of Coxey's "Army" captured a freight train at Troutdale and were in turn captured by Federal cavalry at Arlington, 120 miles to the east. The wild and wide-open days of Cheyenne, Laramie, and Pocatello are now only memories, yet fragrant ones, redolent of coal smoke and hot valve oil.

When the clouds scurry across the moon and the wind sweeps through the unchanging sage, who can say but that the ghosts of the old days along the U. P. trail make their phantom runs, vanishing when the pink tints of dawn streak the eastern skies and drive the shadows from the purple ridges.

UNION PACIFIC ENGINE No. 119, star performer at the Golden Spike ceremonies, pushes two flat cars across a bean-pole trestle on the climb to Promontory, Utah. In the rear of the rig standing near the base of the structure, lower left, can be seen the portable darkroom of the pioneer photographer who exposed the glass plate to capture this lovely scene for posterity. (Courtesy of Union Pacific Historical Museum)

PETERSON STATION was a telegraph office on the Union Pacific, located in the Weber Canyon in Morgan County, Utah. This old photo from the archives of the Latter-day Saints Church shows Union Pacific's No. 66, a 4-4-0 with oil light and diamond stack, standing at the Peterson depot. Daniel Gamble, the first Union Pacific telegraph operator in Ogden, later took charge of this office and remained here until his retirement. (Courtesy of the Church of Jesus Christ of Latter-Day Saints)

GOLD SPIKE ACTOR. Engine 119 of the Union Pacific headed the special train from the east that touched pilots with the Central Pacific's JUPITER upon completion of the first transcontinental railway at Promontory, Utah, on May 10th, 1869. This photo of the 119 was reputedly taken on the day of the great celebration.

SAGEBRUSH EPIC. This view, a different angle shot from the photographs customarily used to depict the historic event, shows Engine 119 of the Union Pacific facing the Central Pacific's JUPITER at the Gold Spike ceremonies at Promontory, Utah, on May 10th, 1869. Charles R. Savage, the noted Utah photographer, accompanied Mormon Bishop John Sharp from Salt Lake City to Promontory and recorded the action of the day for future generations. (Courtesy of Southern Pacific)

RAILROADERS' EXCURSION. After the Golden Spike was tapped home at Promontory in 1869, the Union Pacific ran a special train up Weber Canyon, east of Ogden, to show the visiting Californians a bit of Utah scenery. The group of visitors and celebrities are shown here at Devil's Gate bridge, posed on a flat car fitted with plank seats to serve as an observation car. The coach ahead of the platform car is lettered "Central Pacific Railroad of California" and is probably the private car of Leland Stanford, president of the Central Pacific. (Courtesy of Union Pacific Railroad)

JUNCTION ON THE OREGON SHORT LINE at McCammon, Idaho, as it appeared about 1892. The main line west from Granger, Wyoming, met the branch from Ogden here on the sage brush plains, then followed the old Utah & Northern route toward Pocatello. Heading the freight train shown here is Oregon Short Line's No. 998, a diamond stack 4-6-0 coal burner. (Arthur Petersen collection, courtesy of H. R. Griffiths, Jr.)

OREGON RAILWAY & NAVIGATION COMPANY TERMINAL pictured here was located at Albina, Oregon, now a part of metropolitan Portland. This photo of the roundhouse there was probably taken in the late 1880's, and shows a pair of cap-stacked eight-wheelers. No. 81, standing to the right of the "armstrong" turntable, was built by Baldwin in 1883. The Albina terminal is still in operation, now a part of the Union Pacific system. (Courtesy of Union Pacific Railroad)

U. P. TRAIL, winding into the Northwest over the Oregon Short Line, connected with the Oregon Railroad & Navigation Company at Huntington, Oregon, to forge the link over the Blue Mountains and down the Columbia River to Portland. Here, in classic simplicity, is American Standard No. 35 of the O. R. & N., heading two coaches and a caboose at Bingham Springs, Oregon. The 4-4-0 was built by Baldwin in 1882. (Moorhouse photo, courtesy of University of Oregon)

PENDLETON, OREGON, TERMINAL of the Oregon Railway & Navigation Company is shown in this early photograph; the town has been noted for many years for its famed Pendleton Roundup, a rodeo in the old Western fashion. Engine 59, sporting a set of four-point buck horns on her oil lamp, was a 4-4-0 built by Manchester Locomotive Works in 1883. At the left is the three-stall roundhouse, with the nose of Engine 51 showing through the door beyond the turntable. A sister engine of No. 59 was the O. R. & N. No. 61, later renumbered 67, which blew up at Whitman, Washington, in 1910.

Oregon Short Line Album

O. S. L. No. 450 was a 4-4-0 built by Grant Locomotive Works in 1887, equipped with slide valves and 63 inch drivers. Photo taken at Glenn's Ferry, Idaho.

O. S. L. No. 906 was a 4-8-0 built by Cooke in 1899 and had 55 inch drivers. Photo at Pocatello, Idaho, in 1904.

O. S. L. No. 940 was a 2-8-0 built by Cooke in 1897. She had 51 inch drivers and a boiler extending through the cab.

O. S. L. No. 722 was a 4-6-0 built by Cooke in 1899 with 57 inch drivers. Photo taken at Pocatello in 1904.

O. S. L. No. 770 was a 2-6-0 built by Baldwin. This photo shows the compound Mogul and crew at Montpelier, Idaho, in 1901. Note the elk antlers on the cupola of the caboose.

O. S. L. No. 560 was an 0-6-0 switch engine built by Baldwin in 1901, with 51 inch drivers. Photo at Pocatello in 1904.

(All six photos, courtesy of Henry R. Griffiths, Jr.)

WONDERFUL ACTION SHOT, taken in 1904 by that master rail photographer, Fred Jukes, graphically depicts the rigors of running an engine in cold weather. Union Pacific's No. 1653 is enveloped in a white cloud of steam as she labors west out of Rawlins, Wyoming, with 2,000 tons, bound up the 29 miles of 1% grade to Creston, summit of the Continental Divide. Compound engines of this type were called "slam-pounds" by the crews, and their habits of leaking steam earned them many other nicknames, all unprintable! (Courtesy of Fred Jukes)

FROM THE SUNNY SOUTH came this Baldwin 4-6-0 to steam across the plains of Wyoming as No. 101 of the Saratoga & Encampment Railway. Built in 1884, she was formerly No. 145 of the Georgia Rail Road & Banking Company, later becoming Central of Georgia Railroad's No. 1309 before being sold west. This fine shot, detailing the steer horns on her headlight and her outboard engine truck, was taken at Walcott, Wyoming, in 1908, the year in which she was acquired by the short-line Saratoga & Encampment Railway Company. (Courtesy of Fred Jukes)

ROCKY RAMPARTS OF WEBER CANYON dwarf these three Union Pacific 4-4-0's, posed on the bridge at Devil's Gate, Utah, about the time the first transcontinental railroad was completed. The two side-door cabooses, innocent of cupolas, are numbered 10 and 14; each bears the legend, "U. P. R. R. UTAH DIV." The locomotive coupled next to the waycars is the Union Pacific's No. 120, but the numbers of the other engines are not visible. (Courtesy of Union Pacific Railroad)

The Trail To Santa Fe.

On October 30th, 1868, a spade turned a sod of rich Kansas earth at Topeka, the beginning of a colorful railway that has firmly entwined its history with that of the great American Southwest. The steel rails of the Atchison, Topeka & Santa Fe invaded a region rich in historic lore and in their own way contributed to the development of the vast plains region.

The Santa Fe, organized by Colonel Cyrus K. Holliday, was destined to reach the shores of the Pacific and on its westward march it followed in the steps of a ghostly army of adventurers. Roving bands of Indians, Spanish explorers, and daring hunters and trappers had trampled the path ahead of the rails. The smoke of Santa Fe engines drifted over campsites where the mountain men had broiled hump ribs of buffalo, and the clang of spike mauls rang in rocky gorges that had echoed the tramp of Coronado and Cabeza de Vaca. The rumble of freight trains silenced the creaking caravans of ox-drawn wagons that crawled laboriously into ancient Santa Fe, through the wastelands ruled by the Bents and St. Vrains.

The Santa Fe brought other things to the Southwest in addition to rapid transport. It ushered in Fred Harvey and his famous chain of eating houses, complete with feminine influence and enforced manners. Cattle baron or cow-puncher, banker or boomer brakeman, all donned coats before entering a Harvey House dining room.

The Santa Fe, sweeping across the Kansas plains, followed the Arkansas River into La Junta, Colorado, then swung southwest into the drainage of the Rio de Las Animas en Purgatoire, locally corrupted into the "Picketwire". Reaching Trinidad, the rails turned south across the border into New Mexico. The climb to the line took the road over Raton Pass on the old toll road grade kept by "Uncle Dick" Wooton. Civil Engineer Ray Morley edged out a Denver & Rio Grande survey party by a slim margin to stake the Santa Fe's claim to the Raton route. A temporary switch-back carried trains over the hump while the summit tunnel was being bored.

Work from the New Mexico State Line into Las Vegas was carried on by the subsidiary New Mexico & Southern Pacific Railroad, the section being opened for operation on July 4th, 1879. This same company laid their iron west, swinging around the Las Vegas Range, the southern tip of the Rocky Mountains. The tracks stretched through Glorieta to Lamy and down the Rio Grande River to Albuquerque, with a branch from Lamy into the ancient pueblo of Santa Fe. This section was placed in service in 1880. This leased company built on south through San Marcial to Deming, the segment between the latter two points being constructed by the Rio Grande, Mexico & Pacific, a concern that also built from Rincon, New Mexico, to the Texas State Line, where the Rio Grande & El Paso took over to push the road into El Paso.

From a junction a short distance south of Isleta, the Atlantic & Pacific Railroad headed west toward the waters of the Colorado River. The Santa Fe controlled the Atlantic & Pacific by stock ownership but the road operated under its' own name until 1897.

West from Isleta, the Atlantic & Pacific headed across western New Mexico, crossing the Continental Divide between Laguna and Gallup. From here the road crossed into Arizona Territory, dropping down to Holbrook and Winslow. Twenty-six miles west of Winslow lay the famous Canyon Diablo, a rocky gorge blocking the path of the A. & P. rails. Freight wagons carted supplies across the desert and construction of a steel bridge over the deep trench was started well in advance of the arrival of the end of track. Bridge gangs labored 15 months to complete the spidery steel structure.

SECOND NUMBER TWO, this Santa Fe beauty was built in the road's Topeka Shops in 1881 at a cost of $8,600. A 4-4-0 with 62 inch drivers, she was named the WM. B. STRONG, in honor of William Barstow Strong, president of the Santa Fe from 1881 to 1889. President Strong was further honored by the road when the station of Waterman, California, was changed to Barstow. Many stations throughout the Southwest were named for officials and employees of the Santa Fe and the Atlantic & Pacific. (Courtesy of Santa Fe Railway)

When the span was completed, Atlantic & Pacific tracks went shining on toward the setting sun. The route carried them through Flagstaff, Williams, Ash Fork, and Kingman until at last the rails dipped down to the mighty Colorado River at a point a short distance below Needles, the terminus of the road in eastern California.

From Williams, the Santa Fe & Grand Canyon Railroad was built north to serve the copper mines around Anita. This company failed before reaching the rim of the great scenic gorge, and a Santa Fe subsidiary, the Grand Canyon Railway, completed the branch in 1901.

The Atlantic & Pacific met the rival Southern Pacific at Needles in 1883. The busy terminal was a typical rough railroad division point. Saloons flourished and living accomodations were deplorable. The intense heat caused a high turnover in operating personnel and a steady stream of boomers drifted in and out. The shops offered ready employment to a multitude of boomer machinists, craftsmen whose mechanical skills were much in demand. When working in Needles, the prudent boomer nut-splitter doused his tools with a bucket of water before attempting to pick them up. The scorching rays of the desert sun heated the metal to a degree that nearly burned the skin. Some of the boomer machinists who put in time in the Needles shops rose to high places. Among these were Herbert S. Wall, later Mechanical Superin-

tendent of the Santa Fe's Coast Lines, and Dan Cunningham, who served as Supt. of Motive Power on the Denver & Salt Lake and later as Master Mechanic for the D. & R. G. W. in Salt Lake City. Other Santa Fe men who served at Needles included Master Mechanic Fred Havil, Shop Foreman Jack Records, and Roundhouse Foreman Jimmy Lawler.

The genus boomer was not restricted to road crews and shop men. The telegraph operators who manned the remote stations migrated as freely as the birds. After a few months at some isolated, sun-baked hell-hole on the desert the average young boomer lightning slinger was ready to pull the pin and ramble off in search of greener pastures. A few hardy souls braved out the lonely vigils at the key and remained to grow whiskers and become settled home guards.

The thin strand of wire lining the track was the life line of the railroad. Over it went the daily flow of train orders and messages, the routine work of train dispatchers and operators. This prosaic flow was sometimes interrupted by urgent demands that rattled from sounders along the line . . . calls for the big hook when derailments or collisions piled up the trains, the tragic messages to next of kin when a trainman slipped under the car wheels. The key helped banish the loneliness of desert duty during hours when the line was clear, and operators chatted and gossiped across the long miles.

HEADED WEST, the early trains of the Atchison, Topeka & Santa Fe rolled along behind graceful American types such as No. 5, the THOMAS SHERLOCK. Named in honor of an early director of the road, she was built by the Taunton Locomotive Works in 1870 and cost the Santa Fe a tidy $5,800. Specifications of the engine included 67½ inch drivers, 15 x 22 inch cylinders, and a total weight of 30½ tons. She remained in service until 1911, going to the scrap pile after 41 years of faithful toil and service. (Courtesy of Santa Fe Railway)

A FLEET OF DESERT RAMBLERS of the Southern Pacific of Arizona attract some Indian admirers, seen beside the tank of No. 10. Engine No. 8 heads out toward the turntable, while No. 6 occupies the second stall in the roundhouse. (Courtesy of Chas. E. Fisher)

Not long after the Atlantic & Pacific steel pushed into Arizona Territory, the Santa Fe, forseeing the rival Southern Pacific's blockade of the California extension at Needles, put another iron in the fire. Ray Morley and a crew of Santa Fe surveyors bundled up their gear and began nosing around the vast expanses of Sonora Province in Old Mexico. The results of Morley's expedition sent President Strong hurrying down to Mexico City to set up a scheme that would carry the Santa Fe rails to a port on the blue Pacific. In 1879 the Sonora Railway project was launched, construction starting on the Gulf of California at the port of Guaymas. Around Cape Horn came a ship loaded with rails, a locomotive, and a number of flat cars.

Gangs of Mexican laborers were employed and by the end of 1880 the grade was completed from Ardilla Island, the terminus point in the bay at Guaymas, north some ninety miles to the adobes of Hermosillo.

More locomotives came around the Horn and trains were in operation to Hermosillo in November of 1881. On October 25, 1882, the road from Guaymas was completed into Nogales, on the Arizona border, where it joined the tracks of the New Mexico & Arizona, a Santa Fe subsidiary that had built down from Benson on the Southern Pacific. Except for the trackage between Benson, Arizona, and Deming, New Mexico, controlled by Southern Pacific, the steel of the Santa Fe now reached

UNCLE DICK. When the Santa Fe's subsidiary New Mexico & Southern Pacific Railroad built in 1878, a steep switchback with 6% grades made it necessary to obtain a locomotive more powerful than any in use on the road. The Baldwin Works obliged by constructing a 2-8-0 saddle tank, acclaimed as the heaviest locomotive ever built when she was completed. The engine was shipped west in dismantled sections, being too heavy for the bridges and trestles en route. The locomotive was assigned No. 204 and was placed in helper service over Raton Pass; she was named the UNCLE DICK in honor of Richens Lacy Wootton, veteran frontiersman who aided Ray Morley in gaining entrance for the Santa Fe into New Mexico Territory over Wootton's famous toll road grade, a coup that headed off the rival Denver & Rio Grande of General Wm. Palmer. (Courtesy of Santa Fe Railway)

from Topeka to the waters of the Pacific.

Over this Mexican road, some 315 miles in length and known as the Ferro Carril de Sonora, a fleet of 4-4-0's built by Rogers and the Rhode Island Locomotive Works wheeled trains through Torres, Ortiz and Llano. The engines of the F. C. de Sonora, in addition to numbers, bore such colorful names as *Arispe, Gen. Riva Palacio, S. Camacho, Yaqui* and *Magdalena.*

After the turn of the century, the Santa Fe and the Southern Pacific got together for a bit of horse-trading, and the old F. C. de Sonora ended up as a portion of the Southern Pacific of Mexico, while the Santa Fe received the Needles-Mojave line, which it had operated under lease since 1884.

About the time that the Guaymas line was completed, the Santa Fe started construction of another line from Pacific tidewater to the east. The California Southern Railroad Company was organized in 1880 and construction pushed on a line from San Diego north and east toward a junction with the Needles line at Barstow, in the Mohave Desert. Actual terminus for the road was at National City, on the famous old Rancho de la Nacional, just south of San Diego. Engineer John Zander and Conductor J. H. McNeil manned the first work train, and soon the grade stretched up along the coast, turning inland to reach Fallbrook at the western slope of the Santa Ana Mountains. Rails laid through Temecula Canyon were swept away in one of the periodic cloudbursts, and the route was relocated, running north to San Juan Capistrano and Santa Ana, thence east to San Bernardino. At Colton, a battle was fought with the Southern Pacific before a crossing of the S. P. tracks could be completed to carry the Santa Fe rails north into San Bernardino.

From Barstow (formerly Waterman) on the line leased from the Southern Pacific, the Santa

CANYON DIABLO, the Devil's Gorge, was located between Holbrook and Flagstaff, Arizona Territory, and was spanned by this spidery bridge erected by the Atlantic & Pacific Railroad. This portion of the present Santa Fe line across the Southwest was opened in 1882, about the time this photo was taken of the high-stacked American Standard and her 3-car, open platform passenger train. These dry canyons and arroyos of the great Southwest became veritable sluices when storms lashed the region, creating flash floods that often disrupted rail traffic. (Courtesy of Santa Fe Railway)

THE COAL CHUTES AT NEEDLES form the setting for this view of Atlantic & Pacific's No. 115, a heavy 4-6-0 built by Baldwin in 1892, Shop No. 16396. The engine has a wagon-top boiler, single stage air compressor, and link and pin coupler. Her engineer and fireman have assumed the classic pose for this photo taken in 1892. (Courtesy of R. P. Middlebrook)

ENGINE 71 OF THE AT-LANTIC & PACIFIC heads a freight train in the Needles yards in 1890, coal smoke oozing from her diamond stack. The 4-6-0, a Pittsburgh product of 1880, bore Shop No. 988 and was equipped with an oil headlight that illuminated the engine numbers stencilled in the box overhanging the lens. The faces of the train and engine crew reflect the changing fashion in facial adornment; the veteran skipper retains the bushy beard popular a decade or two earlier, the enginemen sport mustaches, but the hirsute crop of the three brakemen has fallen before the keen blade of the old straightedge razor. (Courtesy of R. P. Middlebrook)

THE WAIL OF THE ROUNDHOUSE WHISTLE, calling out the wrecking gang, was as common in the Southwest as it was in other regions in the wild and rough days of early railroading. A frightful head-on collision piled these three Atlantic & Pacific ten-wheelers into a tangled mass of wreckage at some unidentified location in the desert country. A fourth locomotive may have been involved, indicated by the cab visible behind the tender at the far left. The crushed and jumbled equipment conveys some idea of the force of impact when these trains met at speed. (Courtesy of R. P. Middlebrook)

70

ATLANTIC & PACIFIC RAILROAD boasted a fine fleet of big 4-6-0 type locomotives for use in the mountains and deserts of the great Southwest. Ten-wheeler No. 64, built by the Pittsburgh Locomotive Works in 1880, is shown here with her engine crew at Needles, California, in the lusty heyday of her career. The year is 1890 and the Golden Age of steam locomotion lies enchantingly across the land. (Courtesy of R. P. Middlebrook)

Fe's California Southern completed the road to San Bernardino, over the noted Cajon Pass. Cajon, Spanish for box, divides the ranges of the San Bernardino and San Gabriel mountains and the rails were completed through the gap in 1885, giving the Santa Fe a terminal on the Pacific within the limits of the United States. The work on the line over Cajon Pass had been done by Mexican gangs on the south end and by Chinese toiling up from the north. In the days of steam, the climb over the 3,800 foot summit was one of the dramatic highlights of Western railroading, with a backdrop of mountain scenery fully as rugged as anything the Rockies had to offer.

The network of Santa Fe trackage radiating south and east from Los Angeles was the result of the acquisition of a number of local railroads, including the Los Angeles & San Gabriel Valley and the California Central. Other lines gathered into the Santa Fe fold in the area were the San Bernardino & Eastern, the Elsinore, Pomona & Los Angeles, and the Riverside, Santa Ana & Los Angeles.

The Santa Fe reached north to San Francisco Bay through the acquisition of several short line roads, invading the home ground of the rival Southern Pacific.

For many years the Southern Pacific had controlled most of the railroads around the Bay area, although several attempts had been made to break their monopoly. On Feb. 20, 1895, the people of the San Joaquin Valley, sparked by leaders from San Francisco, formed the San Francisco & San Joaquin Valley Railway.

Among the leading citizens in the formation of the Valley Road were James D. Phelan, James Flood, Claus Spreckels and the latter's sons, John D. and Adolph B. Spreckels. Work began at Stockton on July 22, 1895, and soon the steel was laid into Fresno. Wild enthusiasm greeted the new road, and the Valley Road's train became known as the "Emancipator." By May of 1898, the rails were into Bakersfield, backed by Santa Fe capital, but the route over the Tehachapi Mountains presented a serious obstacle. Southern Pacific steel occupied the most feasible location, so the Valley Road built

ALBUQUERQUE DEPOT IN 1896. The Santa Fe station force posed in front of the wooden frame structure for this photo, located about the later site of the lobby of the Alvarado Hotel. Note the old style train order signal, placed in "Stop" position. Ticket office, waiting room, and baggage room were located on the ground floor of this building, while the upper floor housed the "AG" telegraph office, station agent's quarters, and the office of the old Aztec Land & Cattle Company. (Courtesy of Santa Fe Railway)

on to Kern Junction and entered into an agreement with the S. P. to use the existing trackage from Kern to Mojave as a joint operation.

On the top end of the Valley Road, the line was extended from Stockton to Richmond and opened for service in 1900. The grand old Columbia River side-wheeler *Ocean Wave* was brought down to serve as the ferry connection between San Francisco and Richmond, a familiar role to the old paddler that had served the Ilwaco narrow gauge line up in Washington State.

The Santa Fe built on into Oakland, utilizing the remains of old "Borax" Smith's California & Nevada, which they re-named the Oakland & East Side. Service over this route was inaugurated in May, 1904. Next step of the Santa Fe was to acquire control of several short line railroads in the redwood region of the northern California coast, the nucleus of the Northwestern Pacific Railroad. In 1928 the Santa Fe sold its stock in this venture to the Southern Pacific Company.

After withdrawing from the Northwestern Pacific operation, the Santa Fe settled down in its established territory in the Southwest and built a reputation for fine passenger and fast freight serv-

ATLANTIC & PACIFIC ROUNDHOUSE at Needles, California, in 1890. The Atlantic & Pacific Railroad built southwest from Kingman, Arizona, and met the Southern Pacific's Mojave-Barstow-Needles line here on the west bank of the Colorado River in 1883. Thirteen stalls can be counted in the engine-house shown here, and the machine shop was located in the east end of the structure, at far right in this photograph. Building on the left, behind the coal chute incline, was the sand house; the stock cars ahead of the gig-topped caboose in the foreground testify to the heavy cattle shipments that rolled out of the grazing regions over the Atlantic & Pacific rails. The station took its name from a group of peaks called The Needles that spired up on the eastern shore of the tawny Colorado. (Courtesy of Santa Fe Railway)

TILED ROOF AND GRACEFUL ARCHES of the San Diego station reflect the influence of the Spanish padres on California architecture. Engine No. 2 of the Santa Fe is pictured here as she appeared in 1915, buckled onto Train 81, the Escondido passenger. The long-barreled 4-4-0 was built by Manchester in 1887, Shop No 1352. (Courtesy of R. P. Middlebrook)

ice. The fame of the Santa Fe's fleet of varnish spread far and wide, heralded by such trains as the *"Grand Canyon Limited," "The Chief," "The Scout,"* and *"El Capitan."*

An interesting sidelight on Santa Fe operations was the wonderful assortment of desert roads that could be reached from Ludlow, California. The Ludlow & Southern Railroad ran a short distance south from Ludlow to serve the Pacific Mines, but the more celebrated Tonopah & Tidewater Railroad extended north from Ludlow to connect with such colorful pikes as the Death Valley Railroad, Tecopa Railroad, and, at Rhyolite, Nevada, with the Las Vegas & Tonopah Railroad and the Bullfrog-Goldfield Railroad. To the north lay the original Tonopah Railroad and the little Silver Peak Railroad, built to serve the mines around Blair, Nevada.

East of Ludlow, the California Eastern connected

with the Santa Fe at Blake, running north to Vanderbilt, while west of Ludlow the rails of the Daggett & Borate left the Santa Fe at Daggett. Further west, the old Randsburg Railroad left the Santa Fe at Kramer, running north to Randsburg and Johannesburg, names reminiscent of the mining regions of South Africa.

Many of the little roads have since passed into oblivion, their ties rotted and the grades eroding back into the desert from which they were scraped, but the Santa Fe steel still pulses with the flow of traffic. Steam no longer blasts through Cajon Pass nor storms over Raton, but the Diesels burnish the rails that old Colonel Holliday envisioned on that blustery October morning in 1868 when he broke the first earth for the road that was to lead to Santa Fe and across the Southwest to the waters of the Pacific Ocean.

ATLANTIC & PACIFIC SHUNTER, Engine 95 shuffled cars in the Needles yard in 1890. Shirt-sleeved throttle jockey Frank Hutt stands beneath the fire pump mounted on this 0-6-0 switch engine. Note the grab iron and footboard extending along the entire length of the goat's tender. While not clothed in the aura of glamor surrounding the high-stepping road engines, humble switchers such as this were the work horses of the railroad in an age when switchmen carried oil lanterns and 12 hours was considered a day's work. (Courtesy of Santa Fe Railway)

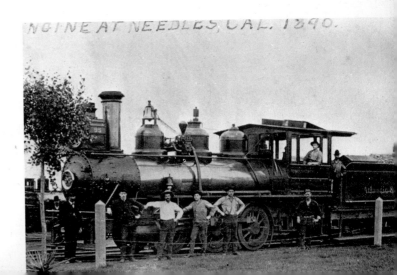

ATLANTIC & PACIFIC FREIGHT TRAIN was captured on the high bridge over Canyon Diablo, Arizona, by the camera of that noted pioneer Western photographer, William H. Jackson. The seven water cars coupled behind the diamond stack engine each support two barrel-shaped tanks, mute testimony to the scarcity of water in the desert regions. The railroad expended a great deal of effort to transport an adequate supply of the precious fluid, so necessary to man and locomotive alike. In many places, the alkali content was so high that the water was practically unfit for use in boilers, causing excessive foaming with the added danger of burning a crown sheet. In later years, treating plants and chemicals helped render this bad water fit for use by the steam locomotive. (W. H. Jackson photo, Library of State Historical Society of Colorado)

TRAIN TIME ON THE SANTA FE at Raymond, California, in 1886. The locomotive, with cap stack of classic design, heads five cars of varnish at the wooden depot, while an omnibus drawn by a span of matched greys and an open-sided horse car await their loads of passengers. Orchards and farms dot the lush flatlands beyond the station buildings and the big wooden water tank. (Courtesy of Santa Fe Railway)

TRAIN NUMBER FOUR of the Atchison, Topeka & Santa Fe halts at Thatcher, Colorado, in 1889. The varnished consist included mail, express, baggage, smoker, day coach, tourist sleeper, and San Francisco, Los Angeles, and El Paso Pullman cars. Her schedule called for the departure from Albuquerque at 1:40 A. M. and arrival at La Junta at 5:45 P. M. Standing by Engine 592 are Engineer George Lehey and Brakeman E. F. Smith, with Fireman Thomas J. Brown on the running board; in the group near the express car are Conductor Ed Stimmel and Brakeman Joseph Bowles. The husky capstacked 4-6-0 kept Tommy Brown busy with his scoop as she burned up the long, hard miles on this run. (Courtesy of Santa Fe Railway)

BRASS HAT'S RESIDENCE, this stone house was the first built in New Albuquerque, New Mexico, for Division Superintendent Parker, shown here with his family. The coming of the railroaders, many accompanied by families, had a leavening effect upon the wild boom towns of the West. The line of the New Mexico & Southern Pacific Railroad was opened for operation from Galisteo (now Lamy) to Albuquerque on April 15th, 1880. After a period of leased operation, it was formally merged with the Santa Fe in 1899. (Courtesy of Santa Fe Railway)

SOUTH OF THE BORDER, Engine No. 10 of the Ferro Carril de Sonora poses for her picture in front of the depot at Nogales, Arizona; that portion of the engine from the sand dome forward is in old Mexico, the remainder of the locomotive is on U. S. soil. No. 10 was built by Rogers in 1881 and bore the name, YAQUI. The F. C. de Sonora was completed from Guaymas, New Mexico, to Nogales on October 25th, 1882, by the Atchison, Topeka & Santa Fe interests, giving the Santa Fe a connection to the Pacific Ocean over 262 miles of track in Mexico.

FERRO CARRIL DE SONORA, the Mexican line built uder Santa Fe control, later passed into the hands of the Southern Pacific system. F. C. de Sonora's No. 13, shown here at Hermosillo, Sonora, in 1903, was a Rhode Island wood burner named the ARIZONA. Built in 1881, she had 59 inch drivers, 16x24 inch cylinders, and carried 125 pounds of working pressure. This locomotive later became No. 64 of the Sud Pacifico de Mexico and was retired in 1928. (Courtesy of R. P. Middlebrook)

WILLIAMS, ARIZONA TERRITORY, was a thriving railroad town on the Atlantic & Pacific Railroad, nestled in the pine-clad foothills of the San Francisco Mountains. The town was named in honor of Old Bill Williams, a colorful trapper and mountain man. From Williams, the Saginaw Southern Railroad ran south toward the Black Mesa country, while the Santa Fe & Grand Canyon Railroad extended north to the rim of the majestic Grand Canyon of the Colorado. The latter road, absorbed by the Santa Fe, carried droves of tourists to view the gorge; the first white visitor of record was Garcia Lopez de Cardenas, one of Coronado's lieutenants who was led to the rim by Hopi tribesmen. (Courtesy of Santa Fe Railway)

LOS ANGELES & SAN GABRIEL VALLEY RAILROAD crew pose with their road's first locomotive in 1885, the year in which the line was placed in operation from Los Angeles to Pasadena, Olivewood, Lamanda Park, and Duarte. Controlled by the Santa Fe through stock ownership, the line was operated by the California Central Railway from 1887 to 1889, then by the Southern California Railway until 1904, when it was leased by the Santa Fe and formally merged with the latter road in 1907. (Courtesy of Southern Pacific)

THE CALIFORNIA LIMITED, crack Chicago-Los Angeles flyer of the Santa Fe, stepping along through an orchard-lined valley behind Engine 54, a smart ten-wheeler. This fancy string of varnish was first placed in operation in the fall of 1892. (Courtesy of Santa Fe Railway)

READY FOR BUSINESS, Engine No. 1, the ten-wheeler CLAUS SPRECKELS of the San Francisco & San Joaquin Valley Railway is shown here after towing Engines 2 and 3 onto the Valley Road tracks on October 2nd, 1895. The graceful 4-6-0 was named in honor of the California sugar king who was instrumental in formation and construction of the line.   (Courtesy of Santa Fe Railway)

SOUTH WITH THE BIRDS, many old-time boomers migrated to warmer climes when the first frosts began to chill the morning air on northern pikes. Charles Harvey, a boomer telegrapher and dispatcher, took this service letter with him when he left the Northern Pacific's Rocky Mountain Division at Missoula, Montana Territory, in October of 1883.

"To Whom Concerned: This will introduce Mr. Chas. Harvey, who has been employed as Ass't. Train Dispatcher on the St. Joe and Western Ry., and recently as manager of the telegraph office of this company at Missoula. Mr. Harvey leaves the employ of this company to accept a position as Train Dispatcher with the Atlantic & Pacific R.R. at Williams, Arizona. Any favors in the way of transportation granted him will be worthily bestowed. Yours truly, A. J. Borie, Trainmaster." Harvey had previously been a night operator on the Union Pacific in 1880, was a dispatcher on the Texas & Pacific in 1884, and was Asst. Chief Dispatcher for the Northern Pacific at Missoula, Montana, in 1889, according to old service letters in the writer's collection.

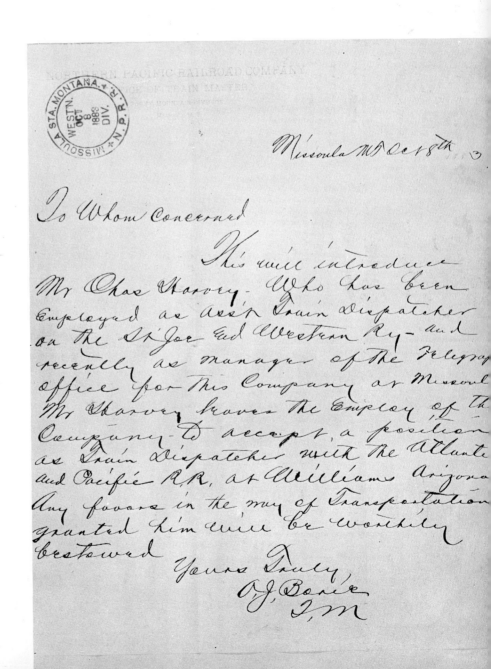

HIGH STEPPER, Engine No. 257 is a good example of the Atlantic types that wheeled Santa Fe passenger schedules around the turn of the century. The fast run of the "Coyote Special," a Santa Fe train chartered by Walter Scott in 1905, captured the fancy of a generation of Americans and is permanently engraved on the pages of Western railroad history. Scott, better known as "Death Valley Scotty," forked over $5,500 for the trip and his special covered the 2,267 miles between Los Angeles and Chicago in 44 hours, 45 minutes. Of the 19 engines used on the trip, 9 were Baldwin Atlantics similar to the 257. The others included 2 Rhode Island ten-wheelers, one Baldwin ten-wheeler, 3 Baldwin Pacifics, and 4 Baldwin Prairie types. (Courtesy of Santa Fe Railway)

FRESNO BOUND, a momentous event in the history of the San Francisco & San Joaquin Valley Railway was the first trip of a through train from Stockton to Fresno, California. Leaving Stockton at 8:07 A.M., the sleek and decorated road engine clipped off the 21 miles to Escalon in 21 minutes and, after frequent stops along the way, rolled the 8-car special into Fresno at 1:30 P.M. Completion of the "Valley Road" broke the Southern Pacific's monopoly and the regular train of the S. F. & S. J. V. was called the "Emancipator" by local residents. At a water stop, Engineer John Armstrong oils around Engine 50, a Baldwin 4-4-0, on the day of the first through trip, October 5th, 1896. (Courtesy of Santa Fe Railway)

SANTA FE'S 327, originally No. 57 of the Southern California Railway Company, was a 4-6-0 built by Manchester in 1887, Shop No. 1319. The depot at Oceanside, California, forms the background for this shot as the oil burner heads up a passenger train scheduled as No. 61.   (Courtesy of R. P. Middlebrook)

HUMP-BACKED 4-4-0, Engine 22 of the Atchison, Topeka & Santa Fe was originally No. 105 of the San Joaquin Valley. Bearing Shop No. 16214, she was built by Baldwin in 1898 and scrapped at Calwa in 1931. This photo shows the fancy stepper at San Bernardino in her declining years.   (Courtesy of R. P. Middlebrook)

LAKE SHORE FLYER. Breeze whips the American flags decorating No. 6 of the Utah Central Railroad, posed here with her proud crew against a backdrop of the rugged Wasatch. The graceful American Standard ran between Ogden and Salt Lake City on the narrow shelf of land bordered by the mountains on the east and by the Great Salt Lake on the west. Mormon toil, faith, and perseverance turned the region from a barren wasteland into an oasis of fertile farms and constructed the railroad to serve the frugal inhabitants. (Courtesy of Central Company, Daughters of Utah Pioneers)

When the Saints Came Rolling In.

A neglected page in the history of Western railroading is the part played by Brigham Young and the Mormons in helping to bring the Iron Horse into the region around the Great Salt Lake.

The people of Utah instigated a movement for a transcontinental railway as early as 1849. Utah's Territorial Legislature petitioned Congress to provide a western rail line in 1852.

When the Union Pacific thrust westward there was great disappointment in Salt Lake City upon announcement that the railroad would not pass through the Mormon capitol. Yet the leader of the Latter-day Saints held no grudge over the matter, but pitched in to help with the Union Pacific construction. In May, 1868, Brigham Young signed a contract with General Reed of the Union Pacific for track work on

SALT LAKE VETERANS, Utah Central Railroad's No. 5 stands at the left while No. 1 raises a black pillar of coal smoke against the snowy Wasatch. The pilots of both engines have been sheathed with metal to ward off drifting snow and the cab of No. 5 has been equipped with a storm curtain to protect her crew from the icy blasts of winter. This photo was probably taken in the yards at Ogden, Utah. (Courtesy of the Church of Jesus Christ of Latter-day Saints)

the pioneer road. The contract covered grading, tunneling and bridge masonry on the section of track from the head of Echo Canyon to the mouth of Weber Canyon. This contract was later extended to cover the grade from the mouth of Weber Canyon to a point near Promontory; grading the Union Pacific over Promontory Summit was completed by gangs employed by Bishop John Sharp.

Young received a large amount of cash for his work, but the Union Pacific could not pay its full indebtedness and Young accepted a reported $600,-000 worth of left-over railroad equipment in settlement for his construction work. If the railroad would not come to the Mormon capitol, Young determined to build a line to connect with it. Even before the final spike of the first transcontinental was pounded home at Promontory, Young went into action. On March 8, 1869, he organized the Utah Central Railroad to construct a standard gauge line between Ogden and Salt Lake City. Brigham Young was president of the Utah Central and all of the stockholders were members of the L. D. S. Church.

Jesse W. Fox was chosen as Chief Engineer and on May 15, 1869, he drove the first survey stakes in the western edge of Ogden, near the present site of the Ogden Union Depot. On the following Monday, May 17th, President Young turned the first

sod and the work of construction was under way. The road crossed the Weber flats and climbed up onto the bench at the western foot of the Wasatch, running in a southerly direction toward Salt Lake City. The grade was laid out on the bottom lands bordering the Great Salt Lake to a point near Kaysville, where it swung in toward the mountains and passed through Farmington and Woods Cross before dropping down into Salt Lake City.

Church leaders and members took up the actual work of building the new road, and soon the 56-pound rail was being laid under the direction of Superintendent Joseph A. Young, a son of President Brigham Young. The locomotive *Black Hawk,* a trim 4-4-0 American Standard of obvious Union Pacific ancestry, began to wheel work trains from Ogden to the end of track. Early records indicate that the first crew consisted of Engineer Robert Bult, Conductor Horatio Hancock, Fireman William Jeffs and Brakeman Albert Gray.

Among the first officials on the Utah Central were Assistant Superintendent Feramorz Little and John W. Young, the latter having charge of much of the track work. Ox teams were employed for grading, but the major problem was a supply of timber for ties and bridges. Crews were set to work hewing ties in Pine and Dry canyons, east of Tooele. These ties were freighted twelve miles to Lake Point, on the south shore of Great Salt Lake, where they were formed into rafts in the shape of cribs, 16 feet wide and 300 feet long. A crew of 20 men then poled these rafts up the lake to a point near Farmington, where teams took over to haul them to the railroad; the men used push poles 16 feet in length to propel these unwieldly rafts. Ties and timbers also came from the headwaters of the Weber and Ogden rivers, and from canyons in Davis County.

A second locomotive was placed in service and by late December of 1869 the track was laid to a point near Bountiful. Early in January, 1870, the hoot of the whistle could be heard in Salt Lake City and Monday, January 10th, was the day set for laying of the final rail.

The citizens were jubilant over the completion of the 37-mile railroad and a huge celebration was arranged. The day dawned cold and frosty, with a heavy fog blanketing the valley, but a crowd of 15,000 gathered near the Salt Lake depot. Shortly after noon the first of two special trains from Ogden, drawn by the locomotive *Black Hawk,* came chuffing into the Mormon capitol. Her crew had been up late the night before, decorating the engine with flags and ribbons and polishing her jacket and brasswork. Engineer Bult was at the throttle and Fireman Jeffs handled the scoop on the special, skippered by Conductor Hancock.

The first train consisted of four coaches, loaded with the brass hats of the road and a number of Union Pacific officials and Ogden business men and church officers Close behind the first train came a second in charge of Engineer Charley Mayard and Conductor John Leavitt, loaded with employees who had helped build the road.

BOARD AND BATTEN STYLE, this depot of the Utah Central Railroad was typical of early stations and was probably located in Ogden, Utah. The neatly-planked platform made smooth going for the youngster mounted on his tricycle. The sign on the depot, below the railroad's name-board, indicates that the structure housed an office of the Deseret Telegraph Company, while the annex in the foreground appears to contain a lunch room. (Courtesy of the Church of Jesus Christ of Latter-day Saints)

A special platform car had been built for the occasion and a large number of dignitaries were seated upon it. These included Brigham Young, Christopher Feramorz Little, and other directors of the the Utah Central; President George A. Smith and 10 members of the Quorum of Twelve Apostles. Representing the Union Pacific were Asst. Supt. Chas. Carr, Master Mechanic C. C. Quinn, Engineer T. B. Morris, and Agents J. McCormick and S. Edwards of the Utah Division. The delegates from the Central Pacific included James Campbell, Superintendent of the Utah Division, Master Mechanic J. E. McEwin, General Freight Agent J. Forbes, and Conductor C. Cornwell. Colonels Hancock and

ORIGINAL PASSENGER STATION of the Utah Central Railroad in Salt Lake City was located at Third West and South Temple Streets. A portion of this depot can be seen over the tank of Engine No. 16, a 4-4-0 type, in this photograph taken in the 1870's. (Courtesy of Union Pacific Historical Museum)

THE SAINTS' HIGHROAD. In the shadow of the Wasatch Range stands Engine No. 1 of the Utah Central Railroad, a wooden passenger coach of Civil War vintage in her wake. The trim 8-wheeler was formerly the Union Pacific Railroad's BLACK HAWK, handed over to Brigham Young and his associates as partial payment of a debt incurred during construction of the Union Pacific's line into Ogden. (Courtesy of Central Company, Daughters of Utah Pioneers)

UTAH CENTRAL RAILWAY No. 14 and a group of the boys posed for this photo at Frisco, Utah, in the 1880's. Frisco, west of Milford, was the station that served the famous Horn Silver Mine. The Utah Central Railway was the combination of the Utah Central Railroad with the Utah Southern Railroad and the Utah Southern Extension Railroad, a consolidation that took place in 1881; the road was later acquired as a part of the Oregon Short Line network. Note the early version of what seems to be a rear view mirror attached on a bracket near the cab window of this Mogul. (Courtesy of Union Pacific Railroad)

Spencer, Major Behham, Captain Hollister, and a number of junior officers from Camp Douglas were on hand to represent the United States Army. Col. F. Anderson, Special Correspondent of the *New York Herald,* was present to record the event for the press. Four bands were standing by, ready to fill the frosty air with martial strains.

After a prayer and a number of addresses, Brigham Young stepped forth to drive the last spike. As if by pre-arrangement, the sun burst through the clouds, beaming down on the bearded old Mormon leader and sparkling on the brass-work of the *Black Hawk.*

T. P. Lewis, a Utah Central track foreman, nipped the tie in place while Young pounded home the final spike. This spike was made by James Lawson, of Salt Lake, from local iron manufac-

tured by Nathaniel V. Jones; the spike maul was a product of the Public Works blacksmith shop. Both maul and spike were chased and engraved by Mr. Reis, a metallurgist of the 16th Ward. Each bore that symbol of Mormon industry, a bee-hive, and the inscription "Holiness to the Lord."

At 2:09 P. M. the final blow was struck, and a salute of 37 guns fired, one for each mile of track. The band blared and the assembled crowd cheered. In that gathering were gnarled and worn pioneers who, only a few short years before, had toiled wearily over desert and mountain to follow their leader to the State of Deseret. Here were members of the valiant handcart companies of 1856 who had arrived in the basin of the Great Salt Lake pushing their earthly belongings in hand-drawn carts. The trail behind them was lined with the

UTAH SOUTHERN RAILROAD'S Engine No. 2 was used in construction when the line was being built south from Salt Lake City to Lehi, Utah, in the early 1870's. The standard gauge 4-4-0 was acquired from the Union Pacific, where she had carried the road number 49. A connection with the Utah Central in Salt Lake City linked Lehi and other neighboring communities with the Union Pacific's main line at Ogden. (Courtesy of Central Company, Daughters of Utah Pioneers)

UTAH NORTHERN RAILROAD'S No. 3 was named the FRANKLIN, in honor of the Idaho town located on the narrow gauge line. The 4-6-0 was built by the Grant Locomotive Works and was decorated with elaborate scroll designs on her tank, polished jacket and dome casings, and an ample supply of brass bands around her boiler. Other early named locomotives on the Utah Northern included No. 1, the JOHN W. YOUNG; No. 2, the LOGAN; No. 4, the UTAH; and No. 5, the IDAHO. (Courtesy of Charles E. Fisher)

graves of their brethren, victims of cholera, hardship and exposure. A number of these brave pioneers had actually frozen to death while attempting to cross the mountains. Who doubts that there were moist eyes in the crowd that watched the Iron Horse roll into Salt Lake, a symbol of rapid transportation over the burning wastes and frozen peaks that the weary parties of Saints had toiled across in their trek to their Promised Land of Zion.

Shortly after the ceremonies, the following message flashed over the wires of the Deseret Telegraph system throughout Utah Territory:

Salt Lake City, Jan. 10, 1870

"To all the Saints throughout the Territory:

"We congratulate you on the completion of the Utah Central. The last rail was laid and the last spike driven at 2 p. m. today. Many thousands were present to witness the ceremonies. Two engines and a number of cars, including two palace cars from the U. P. and C. P. R. R. were in attend-

A DAINTY MOGUL of the narrow gauge Utah & Northern heads a string of flat cars up a rock-rimmed draw near Inkom, Idaho, in the 1880's. The locale is south and east of Pocatello, on the main line of the Utah & Northern running south to Ogden. Primary purpose of the road was to serve the mining and ranching regions of Idaho and Montana, previously supplied by numerous freighting outfits using teams and wagons. Railhead for the horse-drawn freighters had been located at Corinne, Utah, near the mouth of the Bear River. (Courtesy of Union Pacific Railroad)

A LONG WAY FROM HOME, this 2-6-6 Mason engine bearing the lettering of the Denver, South Park & Pacific heads a Utah & Northern passenger train into Garrison, Montana, in 1886. Built in 1879 for the old South Park road, she was originally their No. 22, named the CRESTED BUTTE. In 1885 she was given the number 55, and later sent by the controlling Union Pacific to serve on the narrow gauge Utah & Northern, where this picture was taken. The engine weighed 45,000 pounds, had 13 x 16 inch cylinders, and 37 inch drivers, bearing builder's number 616. There appears to be no record of her final disposition. (Courtesy of Ronald V. Nixon)

ance. Fine celebration. No accident. Grand ball to be given at the Theatre tonight. Love and peace abide with you.

Brigham Young"

The last spike festivities continued far into the night, with the fun-loving Saints dancing in the Theatre. A huge bonfire was ignited near the Arsenal and fireworks displayed in various parts of the city. Stores and business firms had their windows decorated with transparencies, and the office

of the *Deseret News* was plastered with mottoes reading: "The Pioneer Paper welcomes the Pioneer Railroad"; "Brigham Young   Pioneer of the Press, Telegraphy and Railroading," etc. The Mormon's ever-present sense of humor was reflected in another motto reading: "The U. P. R. R. and C. P. R. R. —feeders of the Utah Central!"

From the start, traffic was good on the new road. An item in the *Deseret News* stated that two new locomotives, Numbers 3 and 4, were delivered to the

BATTLING IDAHO BLIZZARDS was no novelty to the hardy crews of the Utah & Northern. Engine No. 85, a 2-6-0, is shown at the Eagle Rock roundhouse in the early days with a pilot plow bolted on her nose and the gangway and tender protected with canvas curtains to ward off flying snow. The 10-stall roundhouse at Eagle Rock blew down in a severe wind in 1886, damaging several locomotives. The shop crew took refuge in the pits under the engines when the structure collapsed. (Courtesy of Henry R. Griffiths, Jr.)

Utah Central in Ogden on February 7th, 1870. These were built by McQueen & Company of Schenectady, New York, at a cost of $12,000. Wages paid the crews were about standard for the era; Joseph G. Young, who had been one of Conductor Leavitt's brakemen, recalled that after three or four years on the road he was promoted to yardmaster in Ogden and paid $2.00 per day.

Joseph A. Young continued as Superintendent of the Utah Central until February 17th, 1871, when he resigned. Feramorz Little was appointed to succeed Supt. Young and held the position until later in the year when he was replaced by John Sharp. In 1873, Sharp was elected President of the Utah Central and continued to serve as General Superintendent. Other officials were Roadmaster John Q. Leavitt, Master of Machinery Henry Brough, and Master Car Builder James Tuchfield.

An amusing incident in the history of the road deals with the naming of one of the stations along the line. When "Uncle Jesse" Fox, Chief Engineer of the Utah Central, was locating the line he found it necessary to cross the farm of "Uncle Jesse" Wood, who tilled the soil at Bountiful. Farmer Wood sought to have Engineer Fox run the line down a little-used wagon road that bordered his property, rather than cut through his fields. An argument ensued, but since both were good Mormons, they agreed to let "Brother Brigham" make the final decision. Engineer Fox presented the case and Young asked him how Farmer Wood's disposition was in regard to the matter. Fox replied that Wood had been very cross about the affair. Young then directed Fox to locate the line as originally planned and ordered that the depot erected there to serve the community of Bountiful be named Woods Cross, and the station bears the name to this day.

The Utah Central provided more than a connection from Salt Lake City to the outside world. It formed the first link in a rail network that radiated from the stronghold of the Saints. Built without aid from outside capital and without help from the Government, the road was a monument to the laboring men of Utah and the leaders of their church who made it a reality.

SNAKE RIVER BRIDGE supports a wonderful Mogul of the old Utah & Northern Railway at Eagle Rock, now Idaho Falls, Idaho. The narrow gauge motive power of the line included several locomotives obtained from the Denver, South Park & Pacific. The Eagle Rock roundhouse and shop buildings can be seen in the distance, to the right of the wooden bridge carrying a wagon road over the historic waters of the Snake. (Courtesy of Henry R. Griffiths, Jr.)

PILE DRIVER AT WORK near Logan, Utah, about 1885 is handled by Utah & Northern Railway No. 100, a 2-6-0 with a diamond stack. When the road was first opened in the early 1870's, the Mormon owners would not allow trains to operate on Sundays. (Courtesy of Henry R. Griffiths, Jr.)

Inspired by the success of the Utah Central, the Mormon leaders organized the Utah Southern, which connected with the Utah Central in Salt Lake and was built south to Payson, Utah. Ground was broken for this road near the Old Fort Block in Salt Lake's 6th Ward on May 1st, 1871, and by 1879 the line had reached Juab. From that point, the Utah Southern Extension Railroad built on to Milford and up to the silver mines at Frisco, Utah, completing this project in 1880. The three roads were consolidated as the Utah Central Railway in 1881, later coming under Union Pacific control.

Another Utah road completed in 1880 was the narrow-gauge Sanpete Valley Railroad, a 30-mile pike built from Nephi to Wales, Utah, by an English outfit to serve their coal mines.

From Sandy, on the Utah Southern, two other short lines were built to tap Utah's mineral resources. The Bingham Canyon & Camp Floyd Railroad built 20-odd miles of 3-foot gauge track west to the copper mines around Bingham City. Promoted by C. W. Scofield and George Goss, the line had 4 engines and handled heavy ore traffic; it was acquired by the Rio Grande Western in the mid-1880's and was standard-gauged in 1900.

East from Sandy ran the picturesque Wasatch &

UTAH & NORTHERN RAILWAY purchased six Consolidation type engines from the Rhode Island Locomotive Works in 1886, numbering them 260 to 265. They had 37 inch drivers, 16 x 18 inch cylinders, and each weighed 61,900 pounds. These six locomotives were sold to the narrow gauge Denver, Leadville & Gunnison Railway, the successor to the Denver, South Park & Pacific, and retained their Utah & Northern numbers when placed in service in the Colorado mountains. Later they bore the lettering of the Colorado & Southern, and were renumbered C. & S. 57 to 62. One of this class, the former Utah & Northern No. 263, is now on permanent display at Idaho Springs, Colorado. The 265, shown here, was scrapped in 1927. (Courtesy of Arthur Petersen)

AMERICAN FORK RAILROAD served the rich mining region located up the American Fork Canyon, running from Sultana, Utah Territory, to a connection with the Utah Southern Railroad at Lehi. Built to a gauge of 3 feet, 6 inches, the road pierced a rugged chunk of terrain and had exceptionally heavy grades and sharp curves. A Fairlie type locomotive was the original motive power used on the line, the bulk of the early traffic consisting of ore and bullion from the famous old Miller Mine. The ONWARD, shown here, was the first engine of her type to be constructed by William Mason in his Mason Machine Works, located in Taunton, Massachusetts. (Courtesy of Charles E. Fisher)

Jordan Valley, a narrow gauge line that reached Granite in May of 1873, Fairfield Flat in September of 1873, and extended to Alta in 1875. Alta, now a famous ski resort, was then a booming mine town. The steep climb up Little Cottonwood Canyon taxed the power of the road's 4 engines. The maximum grade was 287 feet to the mile, with one continuous 3-mile grade of 250 feet to the mile. Nearly 8 miles of snowsheds had to be built to protect the line from heavy snows that blanketed the windswept Wasatch. The road was nearly 20 miles long and did a heavy ore business until the Alta mines began to play out. In the 1880's the section from Granite (now Wasatch) to Alta was abandoned but the lower portion was used to haul granite from the big quarry for use in Salt Lake City. The Wasatch & Jordan Valley was also promoted by Scofield and Goss.

Another narrow-gauge pike connecting with the Utah Southern at Lehi was the nearly-forgotten American Fork Railroad. Work on this 3-foot, 6-inch gauge line started in May, 1872, and the 30-pound rail was pushed up the steep canyons to Sultana. The American Fork carried heavy loads of ore and bullion from the big Miller Mine, and also served other mines in this mineral-rich district. The first locomotive was reportedly a Fairlie type. Mason Machine Works of Taunton, Massachusetts, built an 0-4-4 type for the road and this engine was named the *Onward*. She was reputed to be the first engine of her type constructed by Mason. The road also

AMERICAN FORK CANYON presented some of the most awesome terrain encountered in western railroading. The narrow gauge trackage of the American Fork Railroad, some 21 miles in length, was built up this canyon in 1872 to serve the mines around Sultana, Utah. Before it was abandoned in 1878, the scenery along the line was recorded by the camera of C. R. Savage, pioneer Salt Lake City photographer, and the views attracted tourists in numbers; many excursion trains passed through this steep gorge and under the overhanging cliff, a major point of interest on the road. (C. R. Savage photo, Denver Public Library Western Collection)

owned a 17-ton Porter, Bell & Company locomotive with 6 drivers, 12 x 16 inch cylinders, and capable of hauling 47 tons up the maximum grade of 297 feet to the mile. In addition to ore and mining traffic, the little American Fork road ran many excursion trains, loaded with passengers eager to see the scenic wonders of the rugged canyons. The line was abandoned in 1878, the mines having depleted the ore veins that had been its lifeblood.

While the mining roads were tapping the mineral wealth of the Wasatch ranges, the narrow gauge Salt Lake, Sevier Valley & Pioche Railroad was busy grading a line west from the Mormon capitol around the south end of the Great Salt Lake. Projected by Generals P. E. Connor and E. M. Barnum, this road graded and bridged about 20 miles to Lake Point, but ran into financial difficulties and was not put into operation. In 1874 the road passed into the hands of a group of influential Mormons headed by John W. Young and was reorganized as the Utah Western Railroad, with the intention of extending to Stockton, in Tooele County. The new company soon had 20 miles of track laid, operating the road with 1 locomotive, 2 passenger cars, and 18 freight cars. This line was later acquired by the Oregon Short Line; at one time in its history it was named the Utah & Nevada.

Other interesting short lines in Utah included the narrow gauge Summit County Railroad, formed in 1873 by W. N. Riker and W. W. Cluff of Coalville and LeGrand Young of Salt Lake, and the narrow gauge Pleasant Valley Railroad, which built about 60 miles of track from Provo to the Pleasant Valley coal mines, later forming a part of the Rio Grande Western. Another Utah ore road was the Salt Lake & Western, built in 1874-75 from Lehi Junction to the mines in the Tintic district and used for moving gold, silver, and iron ore; it later was acquired by the Oregon Short Line about 1883.

Probably the best known rail line constructed under Mormon influence was the Utah Northern Railroad, extending from the Salt Lake Basin across Idaho to a connection with the Northern Pacific in Montana. The Utah Northern was organized August 23, 1871, and started construction on a 3-foot gauge road between Brigham, Utah, on the Central Pacific to Logan, in Cache County, Utah. Under the guidance of President John W. Young, the line was completed to Logan on January 1st, 1873. By May, 1874, the little pike had stretched across the border into Franklin, Idaho, slightly over 60 miles. Work had also been carried on south of Brigham, and the rails entered Ogden on February 8, 1874. A connection had also been made with the Central Pacific at Corinne, the historic transfer point on the broad Bear River Flats, by a branch from the Utah Northern's main stem at Lake, Utah.

There was much activity in the mines of Idaho and Montana at this time, and from the Corinne terminal a constant stream of freight wagons had been struggling north, heavily laden with supplies for the interior region.

On May 1, 1874, the first through train set out for Franklin from Logan and, although it was a

RIO GRANDE WESTERN passenger train, headed by Engine 54, stands at the Salt Lake City depot in this photograph by the renowned C. R. Savage. The road had been broadened to standard gauge when the polished ten-wheeler posed for this portrait. The husky 4-6-0 was a product of the New York Locomotive Works, located in Rome, New York. A number of narrow gauge engines used on the Rio Grande Western were acquired second-hand from the Denver & Rio Grande, along with a ten-wheeler from the Denver Circle and a number from other narrow gauge pikes in Utah. (Courtesy of Denver & Rio Grande Western Railroad)

UTAH & NORTHERN MOGUL No. 11 as she appeared with a mixed train at Logan, Utah, about 1885. The building with the smoke-jacks in the left background is the Logan roundhouse. Note the gent with the derby supporting his high-wheeled bicycle on the station platform. (Courtesy of Henry R. Griffiths, Jr.)

freight train, Brigham Young, Erastus Snow, and other Mormon dignitaries were aboard. A derailment caused a long delay and the Saints grew tired of waiting and returned to Logan. With the advent of the Utah Northern into Franklin, that settlement became the terminus of the freighting industry, and warehouses, homes, and stores sprang up around the depot. In January, 1878, the road was completed across the flats into Preston, Idaho.

Old-timers recall that the little engines frequently had to double the hill into Preston, and that it was not uncommon for the first cut to break in two and run back down the grade to crash into the rear portion of the freight train.

The through trains were locally called the "Flying Dutchman," and while they made regular stops at Franklin and Battle Creek, they passed across the rabbit brush flat at Preston with a hoot and a clatter.

UTAH'S BUCOLIC CHARMS were enhanced by the passage of this delightful little string of varnish through the green meadows nestled under the towering rim of the Wasatch. Engine No. 15, an American Standard type, and her three cars posed for this view on the Salt Lake & Ogden Railway near Farmington about 1898. The standard gauge line was chartered on St. Patrick's Day, 1896, and in October of the same year took over the Great Salt Lake & Hot Springs Railway, a short line that had become enmeshed in financial difficulties. The Salt Lake & Ogden Railway later became the Bamberger Railroad, recently abandoned after years of extensive local passenger and freight business. (Courtesy of Henry R. Griffiths, Jr.)

STEEP AND CROOKED, the 3-foot gauge steel of the Uintah Railway wound around sixty-six degree curves and climbed grades exceeding 7 per cent. This line operated from Mack, in the western border region of Colorado, to Rainbow, Utah, the traffic consisting mainly of gilsonite with occasional shipments of sheep and cattle. In this early photograph by Kennedy, a Shay and a helper battle up the tortuous climb around a hair-pin curve. (Courtesy of E. H. Owen, American Gilsonite Company)

SALT LAKE & LOS ANGELES RAILWAY'S Engine No. 2, a 4-4-0, was built by the Rhode Island Locomotive Works and is shown here in the yards at Salt Lake City. Chartered in 1891, the road was opened between Salt Lake City and Saltair Beach in February, 1892, and enjoyed a heavy volume of passenger traffic, carrying Salt Lake City residents to the pleasure resort at Saltair Beach. The fiscal year ending in April, 1905, saw 235,000 passengers chalked up on the books for a neat $50,000 passenger revenue, in addition to $23,000 worth of freight traffic. This road later became the Salt Lake, Garfield & Western Railway. (Courtesy of F. D. Fellow)

When a resident of the scattered village had a letter to mail, he placed it in the split end of a long stick and took a stand beside the track. A member of the train crew would deftly snatch the letter as the train rumbled by.

When Battle Creek was made a division point around 1881, the settlement enjoyed quite a boom. The Utah Northern established a repair shop there, and erected an eight-stall roundhouse to shelter the narrow gauge power.

Although the road was constructed by local people and largely through the efforts of the Mormon Church, it proved costly to operate and soon fell upon hard times. In 1878 the line fell into the hands of Jay Gould, Sidney Dillon, S. H. H. Clark, and others, acquired through a foreclosure sale, and was reorganized as the Utah & Northern. With the coming of Gould's capital, work was pushed on the northern extension and the rails reached Eagle Rock, Idaho, in April of 1879. By May 9th, 1880, the crews were spiking home rails in Monida Pass, crossing the Montana border at an elevation of

UNIQUE POWER, the Uintah Railway's No. 50 was one of two engines of this type built for the road by Baldwin. Ordered by Lucien C. Sprague, general factotum of the Uintah line, they were the only 2-6-6-2 tank type narrow gauge Mallets in the United States. After the Uintah operations shut down, these two engines were sold to the Sumpter Valley road in Oregon, later going to Guatemala when the Oregon lumber pike was abandoned. Their specifications included 15 x 22 inch cylinders, 42 inch drivers, and 210 pounds of working boiler pressure. Their side tanks carried 2,800 gallons of water and the bunkers at the rear of the cabs held 9,000 pounds of coal; the Sumpter Valley removed the side tanks and provided the Mallets with regulation tenders. (Courtesy of E. H. Owen, American Gilsonite Company)

DESERET SPEEDSTER, this high-stepping Atlantic type is Oregon Short Line's No. 856, heading Train No. 19 at Salt Lake City about 1912. Note the cinder trap and drain pipe extending down from the bottom of the smokebox. The big 4-4-2 is equipped with automatic coupler, dynamo, and electric lights, but still sports a wooden stave pilot. (Courtesy of Henry R. Griffiths, Jr.)

6,823 feet. Work was continued and the line reached Silver Bow, Montana, in October of 1881 and built on into Butte, arriving there on December 21st, 1881. In the following year the road was completed north to Garrison, Montana, creating a 466-mile system between there and Ogden, including branch lines.

Under the Gould regime, new power was acquired, including a number of Brooks locomotives, so notorious for their poor steaming qualities that they were called the "cold water Brooks" engines. A number of engines and cars were also sent out from the Denver, South Park & Pacific Railroad in Colorado, and some of this South Park equipment figured in the bad wreck at Dry Creek Station on May 12th, 1885. A freight, heading into the siding, attempted to couple into a string of South Park flat cars loaded with rail, but the coupling did not make and the cars ran out the south end of the siding and off down the main line. They collided with a doubleheader struggling up the grade from the valley of Camas Creek with tragic results, killing Firemen Keitch and Clask and scalding Engineer Flood badly. So great was the impact that some of the rails from the flat cars penetrated the boiler of Engine 55, the leading locomotive of the doubleheader.

The story of the last days of the Utah & Northern has previously been recounted in this work, in the chapter dealing with the Union Pacific and Oregon Short Line roads. When the Oregon Short Line took over and the gauge was widened to standard, the West lost one of its most colorful slim-gauge pikes.

RIO GRANDE WESTERN tracks threaded the canyon of the Grand River in their passage from western Colorado into Utah. In this William H. Jackson photo, a string of varnish fogs along under massive rock escarpments of the desolate region. Originally a narrow gauge when built in 1883, the line was widened to standard gauge around 1889 and became a part of the Denver and Rio Grande Western Railway. (W. H. Jackson photo, Denver Public Library Western Collection)

THE SANPETE VALLEY RAILROAD, chartered in 1873, was the project of an English company to supply an outlet for their deposits of coking coal. The narrow gauge line was built in 1880, and extended 30 miles from Nephi, Juab County, to Wales, Sanpete County, Utah. At one time, the operations were under the direction of Superintendent Simon Bamberger. The road was reorganized as the San Pete Valley Railway in 1893 and was extended from Wales to Morrison, Utah, about 20 miles; a branch 6 miles long was also built from Nebo Junction to Cooper. The road was widened to standard gauge in July of 1896. Engine 50 of the San Pete Valley was a 2-8-0 with a cap stack and slide valves. Note the unusual coupler for link and pin equipment mounted above her stave pilot. (Don Roberts collection, courtesy of H. H. Arey)

CASTLE GATE, UTAH, was a prominent landmark on the old Rio Grande Western main line. This view of the towering rock formations guarding the narrow passage was captured by the camera of William H. Jackson. The rails of the Rio Grande Western cross the wooden truss bridge at lower right before threading their way through the rocky canyon. (Courtesy of State Historical Society of Colorado)

SACRAMENTO VALLEY RAILROAD was the first rail line in California, incorporated in 1853. The road ran from Sacramento to Folsom, near the forks of the American River. It began life as a 5 foot broad gauge, later reduced to the standard 4 feet, 8½ inches. From its terminus at Folsom, the California Central connected for Lincoln, the Sacramento, Placer & Nevada Railroad thrust east to Auburn, and the Placerville & Sacramento Valley Railroad ran over to Latrobe and Shingle Springs. The Central Pacific acquired the Sacramento Valley Railroad in 1865. The 4-4-0 shown here was Sacramento Valley's No. 3, named the L. L. ROBINSON, a product of the New Jersey Locomotive & Machine Company; built in 1855, she blew up at Folsom. The man standing by the tender is reputed to be Theodore D. Judah, Chief Engineer of the pioneer California rail line. (Courtesy of Southern Pacific)

Short Line Album.

The vast region stretching from the crest of the Rocky Mountains to the shores of the Pacific Ocean was bound by a network of major rail lines, rich in history and humming with activity. Yet perhaps the greatest charm lay in the numerous little railroads that flourished in the area, informal to a marked degree in many of their operations.

Time in its flight saw these short lines rise and fall, the victims of mergers or sad abandonments, and often too little remains to mark the sites where their engines spewed cinders in a happier day before the gasoline motor invaded their peaceable kingdoms. Their reasons for existence were many and varied. Some were built in fierce outbursts of civic pride by aroused citizens, indignant because of the treatment

MILL VALLEY & MT. TAMALPAIS SCENIC RAILWAY was a standard gauge road slightly over 8 miles long, constructed from Mill Valley to a point near the summit of Mount Tamalpais, California, in 1896. Geared locomotives hauled trains loaded with excursionists and sight-seers up this steep pike, dubbed the "Crookedest Railway in the World". The Heisler engine shown here with a string of open-sided cars was called the BULL.

accorded their villages by major railroads. Other short lines were the monuments to ill-starred dreams, the humble remains of grandiose projects headed for far places but destined by Fate to wither before their flowering.

To call the roll of these little roads spread across the land would entail a book in itself, but this chapter attempts to catch a fleeting glimpse of a number of them, together with their locomotives, trains, and crews. Lack of space has caused a number of lines to be omitted from the photo section, including such colorful pikes as the copper-hauling Iron Mountain Railway, whose 3-foot gauge rails ran out of Keswick, California . . . the Ione & Eastern Railroad, the Sunset Railroad out of Gosford, the narrow gauge Sierra Valleys Railway into Mohawk, the Bucksport & Elk River Railroad of logging fame, and a host of other roads operated in the Bear State.

Arizona's mines gave birth to such pikes as the Clifton & Lordsburg, the Arizona & New Mexico,

the Arizona Mineral Belt, and the slim-gauge United Verde & Pacific Railway.

Logs from the virgin forests spawned such Washington rail lines as the Natches Pass Railroad, the Port Angeles Pacific, and the Tacoma Eastern, along with numerous private logging roads. Idaho, Oregon, and California hosted equal numbers of these prime movers of logs and lumber.

The deserts of Nevada and the Southwest played the harsh host to such roads as the glamorous Virginia & Truckee, the Tecopa Railroad, the Barnwell & Searchlight, the Eureka & Palisade, the Nevada Central, and the Ruby Hill Railroad.

The borax trains of the Death Valley Railroad no longer whistle into Biddy McCarty Junction and the smoke from the 4-4-0's of the Silver Peak Railroad into Blair, Nevada, faded long ago. Of all the short lines that webbed the valleys and mountains, few remain, and the Pacific West lost a portion of its color and romance with their passing.

SAN FRANCISCO & SAN JOSE RAILROAD was constructed between the points named in its corporate title during the turbulent days of the Civil War, the line being completed into San Jose on January 16, 1864. The road and its extension, the Santa Clara & Pajaro Valley, were acquired by the Central Pacific interests in 1868. Engine No. 5 was a noble 4-4-0 built by Cooke in 1864, equipped with 60 inch drivers and 14 x 22 inch cylinders. Originally named the CHARLES McLAUGHLIN, she had been renamed the SAN MATEO when this photo was taken. The engine later became Southern Pacific's No. 5, then 1112, and was scrapped prior to 1896. (Courtesy of Southern Pacific)

CALIFORNIA PACIFIC RAILROAD was incorporated in 1865 to complete an earlier projected line between Marysville and Vallejo, via Knight's Landing, Davisville, and Suisin. River steamboats provided connections to Sacramento and San Francisco. The road was known as the "Cal-P," probably to separate its identity from the Central Pacific, since both roads had the same initials. The "Cal-P" engine shown here was built by William Mason and appropriately named the LONDON, the line being heavily backed by English capital. (Courtesy of Southern Pacific)

SAN FRANCISCO & ALAMEDA RAILROAD was incorporated in 1863 and built from Alameda Wharf to San Leandro, California. In 1869 the line was taken over by the Central Pacific. Engine No. 1 of the San Francisco & Alameda was a 4-4-0 built at Alameda Point by A. J. Stevens in 1866 and was named the J. G. KELLOGG. She was rebuilt in the Central Pacific shops in 1872 and was sold prior to 1878. This photo was copied from a small picture taken in 1866 by S. P. Sanders, a travelling photographer. (Courtesy of David L. Joslyn)

SAN FRANCISCO & OAKLAND RAILROAD, incorporated in 1861, operated this unusual little 4-4-4 type named the LIBERTY. The short line connected Oakland with a pier not far from the location of the present Oakland Mole and made connections at Oakland Wharf on Gibbon's Point with a ferry boat service to San Francisco. The Central Pacific took over the road in 1869 to provide a waterfront connection for the original Western Pacific Railroad built down from Sacramento in 1862. The LIBERTY, shown here, was No. 1 of the San Francisco & Oakland Railroad, built in their shops in 1863 with 54 inch drivers and 11 x 22 inch cylinders, and was gone from the Central Pacific roster after 1871. Note the odd little cast figure on the pilot beam. (Courtesy of Southern Pacific)

LOS ANGELES & SAN PEDRO RAILROAD, incorporated in 1868, was the first rail line in Southern California. The road was completed from Los Angeles to Wilmington in 1869 and was acquired by the Southern Pacific in 1874. Engine No. 1, a tiny 2-2-0 named the SAN GABRIEL, was built by the Vulcan Iron works of San Francisco in 1868; she had 9 x 18 inch cylinders and 62 inch drivers. Records regarding her disposal are rather hazy, one source stating she blew up in 1869 at San Pedro and was not rebuilt, another record indicating she was scrapped in 1876. (Courtesy of Southern Pacific)

NATIVE DAUGHTER, this graceful American Standard was No. 6 of the San Francisco & San Jose Railroad, where she bore the name, CALIFORNIA. This was the first locomotive built by H. J. Booth & Company at their Union Iron Works in San Francisco, the engine being constructed in 1865. The builder's plate, in the form of a shield, can be seen between the mud guards covering her 62 inch drivers; her cylinders had a 16 inch bore with a 24 inch stroke. (Courtesy of Gilbert H. Kneiss)

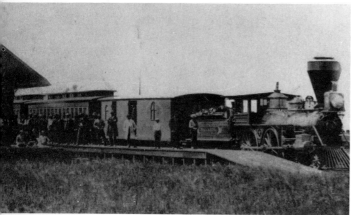

WOODLAND, CALIFORNIA, DEPOT forms the setting for this early view of the California Pacific's Engine No. 5, a 4-4-0 built by William Mason. This engine bore the name, VALLEJO, and carried Mason's Shop No. 250, having been built in 1868. The VALLEJO was later destroyed in a wreck and her parts were incorporated into the Central Pacific Railroad's second No. 121. (Courtesy of Roy D. Graves)

VACA VALLEY'S SECOND ENGINE was a Baldwin 2-6-0 built in 1875 and named the BEN ELY. She had 48 inch drivers, 14 x 22 inch cylinders, and tipped the scales at 55,500 pounds. This Mogul later became No. 2 of the Vaca Valley & Clear Lake Railroad, and after being absorbed into the Central Pacific in 1888, she was assigned Northern Railway No. 1022, later Southern Pacific No. 1500, and was sold in 1892. This view taken at Vacaville shows her in original condition, complete with oil painting on her headlight and equipped with a crosshead cold water pump. (Courtesy of David L. Joslyn)

VACA VALLEY RAIL-ROAD'S No. 1, an odd little 2-2-0 type, bore the name VACAVILLE. She was built by the Vulcan Iron Works of San Francisco in 1867 as the CALISTOGA of the old Napa Valley Railroad. When this photo was taken at Elmira, California, in 1877, she had been acquired by the Vaca Valley and had undergone a rebuilding. The Vaca Valley was later reorganized as the Vaca Valley & Clear Lake Railroad, then passed into the hands of the powerful Central Pacific. (Courtesy of Southern Pacific)

CITY OF PRINEVILLE RAILWAY, one of the few municipaly owned and operated railroads in the west, was built from Prineville Junction to Prineville, Oregon, in 1918. The road followed the canyon of the Crooked River from Prineville to O'Neill's, then climbed up onto a plateau for the level route on to a connection with the joint Oregon Trunk-Union Pacific line at Prineville Junction, north of Redmond. Engine No. 4 was a 2-8-0 built in 1888 by the New York Locomotive Works for the old Oregon Railway & Navigation Co., where she had borne road number 82. The City of Prineville Railway acquired the elderly Rome hog from the Union Pacific in 1940. (Courtesy of Paul A. McMillan)

SAN DIEGO & PACIFIC BEACH RAILWAY transported passengers around San Diego behind this 1-Spot, a gaudy little 0-4-0 steam dummy. This photograph, taken around 1888, shows the steam motor coupled to an odd car that appears to have one end open, in the manner of some of the San Francisco cable cars. The San Diego, Pacific Beach & La Jolla Railway, incorporated in 1894, operated over the standard gauge trackage of the San Diego, Old Town & Pacific Beach Railway; both of these lines were controlled by the same group of investors, headed by Graham E. Babcock. (Courtesy of R. P. Middlebrook)

SAN FRANCISCO & NORTH PACIFIC RAILWAY operated from Tiburon, on San Francisco Bay, to Ukiah, California, serving the coastal counties of Marin, Sonoma, and Mendocino. Several branches offered connections to Donahue, Sonoma, Guerneville, and other points, some tapping the great redwood forests. Engine No. 1, a 4-4-0 built by R. Norris in 1862, is shown here at Sebastopol, California, in 1897. She had originally been No. 2 of the San Francisco & San Jose Railroad, bearing the name SAN JOSE. She later became Northwestern Pacific No. 4. (Courtesy of Roy D. Graves)

ALAMOGORDO & SACRAMENTO MOUNTAIN RAILROAD was a 31 mile standard gauge pike built from Alamogordo to Russia, New Mexico, in 1898, connecting the El Paso & Northeastern Ry. with the rich timber lands of the Sacramento Mountains. The road, along with the Dawson Railway, the El Paso & Rock Island Railway, and other short lines, was controlled by the New Mexico Railway & Coal Company. Engine No. 101, shown here, was a 2-8-2 tank type built by Baldwin in 1898 and later taken into the El Paso & South Western roster. She was converted into an 0-8-0 switcher and later numbered Southern Pacific 1300, scrapped in 1934. Her original dimensions included 46 inch drivers and 21 x 24 inch cylinders. (Courtesy of Southern Pacific)

SANTA CRUZ RAILROAD crew present a study in posed nonchalance for the photographer who recorded this scene for posterity. The JUPITER, a 4-4-0 wood burner, operated on the 3-foot gauge tracks constructed between Pajaro (Watsonville) and Santa Cruz, California, in 1876. Note the odd spark deflector on her stack. The Southern Pacific acquired control of this road in 1882, changing the name to Pajaro & Santa Cruz, and broadening the track to standard gauge. The 21-mile long route later became a part of the Espee's Coast Division. (Courtesy of Southern Pacific)

CARSON & COLORADO RAILWAY, incorporated in 1880, built a 3-foot gauge line over 290 miles long extending from Mound House, Nevada, to Keeler, California. The road connected with the fabled Virginia & Truckee at Mound House. Control of this line passed to the Southern Pacific, who incorporated it into their Nevada & California Railway in 1905. This photo taken in the early 1880's shows the Carson & Colorado's Engine 6 with a mixed freight and passenger consist at the monument marking the state boundary between California and Nevada. No. 6 was a 4-4-0 built by Baldwin in 1882 and scrapped in 1907. She had 41 inch drivers and 14x18 inch cylinders, and was burning wood when this picture was taken. (Courtesy of Southern Pacific)

BOOTH'S UNION IRON WORKS turned out No. 4 for the San Francisco & North Pacific in 1873, and the 4-4-0 was named the GEYSER. She had 14 x 24 inch cylinders and 64 inch drivers. Photographed here at Tiburon in 1900, she is equipped with a cross-head cold water pump and a Janney coupler, with a link pinned into the slotted knuckle. The locomotive was scrapped in 1904. (Courtesy of Roy D. Graves)

SAN FRANCISCO & NORTH PACIFIC'S Engine No. 6, named the CLOVERDALE, was built by the Grant Locomotive Works in 1878. The 4-4-0, shown here at Tiburon, California, in 1900, had 16 x 24 inch cylinders and 63 inch drivers. She later became No. 11 on the Northwestern Pacific and went to the scrap pile in May, 1912. A sister engine, San Francisco & North Pacific No. 7, the PETALUMA, became Northwestern Pacific's No. 12 and lasted until 1926, when she was retired. (Courtesy of Roy D. Graves)

GILA VALLEY, GLOBE & NORTHERN RAILWAY, built in the 1890's, extended for 121 miles between Bowie and Globe, Arizona. The Engine No. 1 was acquired from the Southern Pacific in 1893 and had a colorful background. She was originally Central Pacific's No. 60, the JUPITER, and handled Governor Leland Stanford's special train to the wedding of the first transcontinental rails at Promontory, Utah, in 1869. This photo shows the old veteran with her crew at Globe, Arizona, in 1898, after she had been rebuilt and sold to the Gila Valley, Globe & Northern. The road became part of the Arizona Eastern Railroad in 1910 and the latter road was taken into the Southern Pacific fold in 1924. (Courtesy of David L. Joslyn)

SHETLAND PONY VERSION of the Iron Horse was this tiny H. K. Porter locomotive, an 0-4-2 wheel arrangement with 8x14 inch cylinders and 30 inch drivers. She is shown here in front of the old St. Charles Hotel with a passenger coach while in service on the Albany (Oregon) Street Railway. Built about 1891, the locomotive is reportedly the former Rogue River Valley Railway's No. 1, a 2-4-2 tank type that had been rebuilt and altered when she posed for this photo with Engineer Harry Craw at the throttle around 1895.

SOUTH PACIFIC COAST RAILROAD, a 3 foot gauge line, was built from Oakland to Santa Cruz, California, in 1875. The 80-mile road consolidated with the San Jose & Newark, Bay & Coast, Santa Cruz & Felton, and other narrow gauge lines in the late 1880's to form a system 148 miles in length. The line was leased by the Southern Pacific in 1887 and converted to standard gauge in 1906. Engine No. 1, Baldwin 4-4-0 built in 1875, is shown here with a passenger train at 14th and Webster Streets in Oakland. Her dimensions included 42 inch drivers, 10x16 inch cylinders, and a total weight of 35,000 pounds. (Courtesy of Roy D. Graves)

SOUTH PACIFIC COAST Engine No. 3 in the yards at Alameda Point as the shadows creep across the land. Built by Baldwin in 1876, the 4-4-0 had 42 inch drivers, 12x16 inch cylinders, and weighed 44,300 pounds. She was sold in 1910, becoming No. 4 of the Colusa & Lake Railroad. This photo was taken after the narrow gauge had passed into control of the Southern Pacific; note the Espee's Sunset Route emblem with South Pacific Coast lettering in the background. (Courtesy of Roy D. Graves)

PACIFIC COAST RAILWAY was a California narrow gauge line that operated slightly over 75 miles of 3-foot main stem from Port Harford to Los Olivos, with a branch from Suey Junction to Palmer. One of the ancestral companies in the road's history was the San Luis Obispo & Santa Maria Valley Railroad, organized in 1874. The Pacific Coast Railway was a subsidiary of the old Pacific Coast Company, a concern that controlled coal mines, steamship lines, and the Columbia & Puget Sound Railroad around Seattle, Washington. Engine 106 of the Pacific Coast Ry. was a neat oil-burning 2-8-0, built by Baldwin in 1904. She had 16x20 inch cylinders, 36 inch drivers, and weighed 73,000 pounds. The little Consolidation collided with a gasoline truck in 1938 and was burned.

ENGINEER GUY ROBERTS poses for this view with the National City & Otay Railroad's 6-Spot in 1909. The little 2-4-2 saddle tank was built by Porter in 1888, Shop No. 943, and was named TIA JUANA. No. 6 was equipped with a stave pilot fore and aft, to facilitate operating in either direction without turning. (Courtesy of R. P. Middlebrook)

SAN FRANCISCO & NORTH PACIFIC'S No. 2 was named the J. G. DOWNEY and was an 1870 product of the H. J. Booth works of San Francisco. This photograph shows the pretty 4-4-0 at Tiburon in 1902. Bearing builder's number 14 of Booth's Union Iron Works, she had 14 x 22 inch cylinders and 64 inch drivers. She later became Northwestern Pacific No. 6 when that road acquired the San Francisco & North Pacific, and went to the scrap yard in 1915. (Courtesy of Roy D. Graves)

FIREBOY EYES BUSTLE as No. 11 of the San Diego & South Eastern Railway heads a passenger train at San Diego shortly after the turn of the century. The Mogul, formerly Cuyamaca's No. 1, was built by Porter in 1892 and bore shop number 1375. (Courtesy of R. P. Middlebrook)

NEVADA COUNTY NARROW GAUGE RAILROAD'S Engine No. 3 stands wooded and ready to roll with a passenger train at Colfax, California. Service between Colfax and Nevada City, California, by way of Grass Valley was begun in 1876, one year before Baldwin turned out the neat 4-4-0 shown here. The engine had 44 inch drivers, 11 x 16 inch cylinders, and weighed 42,000 pounds; her brass-bound jacket covered a boiler carrying 140 pounds of saturated steam per square inch. The little iron colt was finally scrapped in 1936. Long-time president of the road was the colorful John Flint Kidder; after his death, the office of president was ably filled by his widow, Sarah Kidder. (Courtesy of Southern Pacific)

SOUTHERN NEIGHBOR, the 173 of the Central Mexicano was a neat 4-6-0 from the Brooks Locomotive Works in Dunkirk, New York. Bearing builder's number 2751, she was constructed in 1897. Many of the locomotives erected by this builder were notoriously poor steamers, the term "cold water Brooks" being used throughout the West to describe them. The 173 has a Belpaire boiler, extending through the cab, and spoked wheels in her tender trucks. (Grahame Hardy print, Author's Collection)

ONLY CONSOLIDATION TYPE on the South Pacific Coast roster, No. 13 was a Baldwin built in 1882 and acquired from the Denver & Rio Grande. This photo, taken at Boulder Creek, California, shows the rear sand dome added by the South Pacific Coast shops and located between her steam dome and cab. The engine later became Southern Pacific's No. 13 and was sold to the Lake Tahoe Railway & Transportation Company, where she retained the same number. (Courtesy of Roy D. Graves)

SOUTH PACIFIC COAST RAILROAD No. 8, a Baldwin product of 1877, was burning wood when this photograph was taken on the flats at Alameda Point, California, in 1881. The 4-4-0 was later converted into a coal burner and was scrapped in 1898. Roy Graves discovered the rare old original of this photo at Downieville, in the Sierra Nevada, and rescued it as it was about to be consigned to a bonfire. (Courtesy of Roy D. Graves)

BALDWIN MOGUL No. 12 of the South Pacific Coast at Newark, California, where the shops of the road were located. Engine 12 and her sister, No. 11, both were built in 1881. In 1906 these two engines were sold to the Nevada & California Railroad, formerly the Carson & Colorado, a narrow gauge line running 299 miles from Keeler, California, to Mound House, Nevada, where it made connections with the noted Virginia & Truckee. Southern Pacific gained control of the Carson & Colorado around 1905. The two Moguls were rebuilt at the Sparks shops in the 1920's, emerging as 4-6-0's, and both were scrapped in 1934. (Courtesy of Roy D. Graves)

TRIPLE HEADER! Three "0-4-0 hay burners" stand ready to highball a mixed freight and passenger consist out of Newark, California, on the 3 foot gauge South Pacific Coast Railroad's branch to Centerville. From the day in 1882 when the branch was placed in service, horses were the only motive power used on it until its abandonment in 1909. It was this Newark-Centerville operation that earned the South Pacific Coast its reputation among local wags as the "one-horse railroad with the two-horse branch." (Courtesy of Roy D. Graves)

YREKA RAILROAD, running between Montague and Yreka, California, was justly proud of OLD BETSY, the road's first locomotive. The 2-4-2 saddle tank was purchased from the Baldwin factory to replace a small locomotive leased from the Central Pacific for construction of the 8.54 mile standard gauge line. Old No. 1 was built in 1889, carried Baldwin serial number 9648, and sported 46 inch drivers powered by 12 x 18 inch cylinders. After serving on the Yreka road, she was reportedly sold to a logging line in the evergreen forests of Washington. Engineer E. F. Dean is shown here in the gangway, with Fireman Jack Frizell leaning from the cab window. On the ground is Mrs. E. F. Dean, wife of the engineer, and their son, Frank G. Dean, who recently retired after many years of service as a locomotive engineer on the Southern Pacific's Siskiyou line. (Courtesy of Siskiyou County Historical Society)

EUREKA & PALISADE RAILROAD extended south from a connection with the Central Pacific at Palisade to the booming silver and lead mines at Eureka, Nevada. The line was incorporated in 1873 and its three-foot gauge rails reached Eureka on October 22, 1875. A year later, with the mines pouring out a stream of traffic, Baldwin built No. 5, the PALISADE, to help handle the flow of commerce. The brass-bound 4-4-0 had 42 inch drivers and 12 x 16 inch cylinders. Earlier locomotives on the road bore such names as EUREKA, ONWARD, and TYBO. (Courtesy of Gilbert Kneiss)

TONOPAH & TIDEWATER'S No. 8 as she appeared at Death Valley Junction, Nevada, in later years. The slide valve Consolidation, Baldwin Shop No. 31791, was built in 1907 and was in use for many years. After the flurry of excitement following the discovery of precious metals in the Bullfrog Hills in 1904, the road settled down to a more prosaic existence, transporting Death Valley tourists and cargos of minerals and base ores, eventually being abandoned. (Courtesy of R. P. Middlebrook)

SAN BERNARDINO & REDLANDS RAILWAY operated this steam dummy on a 3-foot gauge line between the California towns named in its' corporate title. Their first locomotive was an 0-4-4 built by Ricks & Firth in 1887 and their second steam motor was the Baldwin 0-4-2, shown here with Engineer William Simpson at the throttle. This engine was burned in a fire in 1890 and rebuilt, at which time the numbers on the two engines were swapped, hence the No. 1 appearing on the dummy in this photo. The road was leased to the Southern Pacific in 1892 and sold to the Pacific Electric in 1916; abandonment followed not long after the acquisition by the P. E. (Courtesy of Southern Pacific)

SAN DIEGO & SOUTH EASTERN'S No. 15, a 4-4-0, was built by Rhode Island in 1881. This photo shows her as she appeared at San Diego, California, in 1914. Prior to this, she had been No. 1 on the California Southern and No. 3 on the Cuyamaca. (Courtesy of R. P. Middlebrook)

TONOPAH & TIDEWATER was one of the Southwest desert roads that grew out of the periodic mining booms of the region. It connected with the Santa Fe at Ludlow, California, and served the region north to Rhyolite, Nevada, along with such colorful roads as the Bullfrog & Goldfield. Engine No. 4 of the Tonopah & Tidewater is shown here at Ludlow in 1904, steam blowing from her relief valves and cylinder cocks. She was a Baldwin 2-6-0 with a cap stack. (Courtesy of R. P. Middlebrook)

FROM A BATTERED OLD PHOTOGRAPH, torn in two pieces, the skilled hands of Fred Jukes reproduced this rare view of Canadian Pacific Railway, Engine No. 2, an 0-4-0 saddle tank named the EMORY. The early history of this locomotive is clouded, but she apparently was built by Marschuetts & Cantrell of San Francisco about 1879; some sources are of the opinion that Onderdonk used her on his sea wall project in San Francisco before she was shipped to Emory, B. C., early in 1881. She had 14 x 20 inch cylinders and 42 inch drivers, and was nicknamed CURLY by the construction crews. In 1888 the engine was sold to the Hastings Mill Company and worked in the woods, serving logging camps. Her saddle tank was removed and a four-wheel trailer truck put under the rear of her frame. In later years she had a saddle tank and modern domes added, was reconditioned, given a small diamond stack, and placed on exhibition in Vancouver's Hastings Park. (Courtesy of Fred Jukes)

Northwest Memories.

In the century that has elapsed since railroads first began to operate in the Pacific Northwest a great many dramas have unfolded along the iron highways. Tragedy, humor, and heroism have been woven into the legion of tales and true stories handed down in cab and caboose, in yarns spun around pot-bellied depot stoves, and anecdotes recounted whenever railroaders gather.

The men who manned the iron horses were devoted to duty, but they often lightened their labor with good-natured pranks and horseplay. Old Hi was a freight conductor on a crew that batched in their caboose and he was inordinately fond of honey on his morning griddle cakes. His two brakemen were inspecting their train of logs one day when one of them noted a thick stream of amber pitch oozing from

CANADIAN PACIFIC RAILWAY'S western end was constructed by the American firm of D. O. Mills & Company, headed by Darius Ogden Mills of Virginia & Truckee fame. Mills gave financial backing to Andrew Onderdonk, who obtained the contracts for building 212 miles of the road from the terminal at Port Moody, near present-day Vancouver, to Savona's Ferry, British Columbia. Onderdonk obtained a second-hand locomotive from the Virginia & Truckee Railroad to use in construction and this engine became Canadian Pacific Railway No. 1, named the YALE. She was a 2-6-0 built by the Union Iron Works of San Francisco in 1869 as Virginia & Truckee's No. 3, the STOREY. The engine was landed at Emory, B.C., in the autumn of 1880; this photo shows her at Keefer, B. C., in 1885. After the road was completed, she was sent east to the Intercolonial Railway, later passed into the hands of the Canadian National, and was scrapped in 1920. She was the 13th engine built by Booth's Union Iron Works, had 16 x 22 inch cylinders and 43 inch drivers. (Courtesy of H. L. Goldsmith)

a huge log loaded on a flat car. "Looks like old Hi's honey, don't it" he remarked to his companion. In a flash the plot was hatched; a jar identical to the one holding the skipper's honey was procured and filled with the dripping pitch. The substitution was slyly made and the brakemen were rewarded for their efforts the following morning. The caboose was perfumed with the aroma of fresh coffee, sizzling ham, and flapjacks as old Hi heaped his plate and anointed his stack with the amber treasure. The first bite into the pitch-smeared cakes left old Hi with his false teeth firmly trapped in the sticky mess but it did not hamper his wrath nor locomotive powers and early-rising inhabitants were treated to the spectacle of the brakemen fleeing down the track with the angry skipper pounding along in hot pursuit.

A favorite occupation of engine crews in hot weather was the water fight. The game consisted of dousing passing crews with a container of water and in turn, avoiding similar wettings. This called for stealth, intrigue, and alertness. One unlucky fireman had been receiving what he considered more than his fair share of these unexpected dousings and he decided to retaliate. His engine was sidetracked near a water tank one hot afternoon for a meet with a train assisted by several helper engines manned by his tormentors. The fireman climbed up

on the roof of the wooden tank and stationed himself at the control valve. When the drag rumbled past, each fireman was hidden in the gangway, ready to drench their victim with water held in a variety of containers ranging from drinking cups to dope buckets. Not one of them was prepared for the deluge that gushed from the water tank, nearly sweeping them from their cabs, as the tallow-pot manned his tank valve with a vengeance.

Not only did the crews play pranks on each other, but the brass hats were sometimes objects of their rough humor. The trainmaster who was pulling tests on an isolated branch line became the victim of a stunt that won an engineer some measure of fame for his ingenuity. This hogger was at the latch of the last train of the day to pass the spot where the trainmaster was hidden along the track, conducting his efficiency tests. The test consisted of placing a single torpedo on the rail, the explosion of which demanded that the train stop in accordance with the rules; the explosion of two torpedos called only for a reduction in speed for a specified distance. The trainmaster had placed his single torpedo and retired to his hiding place in the bushes, ready to board the train when it stopped and ride back into the terminal. What he did not know was that the engineer had been apprised of his presence by a crew the hogger had met back up the mountain.

The engineer fished a big revolver out of his grip and kept it handy as he wheeled down the grade. When the pony truck exploded the trainmaster's single torpedo the hogger went into action with the pistol, and the echo of the torpedo was followed by the report of the gun. The train slackened speed slightly and roared on down the hill, leaving the puzzled trainmaster to speculate where that second "torpedo" had come from as he angrily tramped down the ties on his long, weary walk to town.

Another trainmaster pulling tests secluded himself in tall grass along the tracks, but a sharp-eyed conductor spotted the official from the caboose as the freight rambled by. The skipper dropped off a message at the next open telegraph office, reporting a body lying near the track at the location where the brass hat was concealed. Headquarters immediately sent a railroad detective and a section gang to search for the "corpse" who turned out to be both alive and disgruntled when he was discovered.

Student railroaders provided a constant source of sandhouse yarns, and the blunders these novices pulled were legion. A freight was holding the main stem at an isolated desert passing track to meet an opposing train and the conductor had walked forward to examine a car in his train. When the meet was made, the freight hogger peeled his throttle and

the freight gained speed so rapidly that the skipper was unable to catch the caboose. This incident took place during the rush business in the war years, and the rear brakie was a student, pressed into the flagman's position due to a shortage of experienced men. As the crummy swept past the conductor, the student was out on the back platform. "Don't go 'way and leave me here!" shouted the conductor. Instead of pulling the air and bringing the train to a halt, the student promptly jumped off and joined the stranded skipper, who was profanely watching the markers on his train vanish down the high iron.

And then there was the student fireman in the same era who was having difficulty in making his oil-burning hog steam. The grumpy runner instructed the lad to look into the firebox, thinking that an accumulation of carbon might have built up in front of the flash wall or burner. Peering inside the firebox, the student got his first look at a flue sheet. "No wonder she won't steam," he gravely informed the engineer. "The oven's all full of holes!"

Train and engine crews played many pranks on student railroaders while educating them in the science of braking or firing and delighted in telling of the boners and blunders committed by the greenhorns. Occasionally a student turned the tables, however, and such an incident occurred when a

CANADIAN PACIFIC RAILWAY No. 7 bore the name KAMLOOPS when she and her engine crew posed for this portrait at Yale, British Columbia, in 1885. The trim 4-4-0 was a Baldwin product of 1884, Shop No. 7274, with the same specifications listed for her sister engine, C. P. R. No. 6, the NICOLA. In 1887 she became Intercolonial Railway No. 185, in 1912 was renumbered 1078, and was scrapped in 1914. The mountains rising in the background are typical of the terrain along the canyons of the Fraser and the Thompson, through whose gorges the thin thread of steel was laid to link British Columbia with the Canadian provinces east of the Rockies. (Courtesy of H. L. Goldsmith)

CANADIAN PACIFIC RAILWAY No. 3 was a Baldwin 2-6-0 named the NEW WESTMINSTER. Outshopped in 1870 with builder's number 2198, she was originally Virginia & Truckee's No. 8, named the HUMBOLDT. She had 16 x 24 inch cylinders, 48 inch drivers, and weighed 55,000 pounds. The Mogul was acquired for the Mills-Onderdonk contracts in British Columbia in May, 1882, and upon completion was taken east, where she became Intercolonial Railway No. 189. In 1913 she became Canadian Government Railways No. 1024 and was scrapped in 1918. This photo shows her at Hope, B. C., in 1885. Two other Baldwin Moguls from the Virginia & Truckee came north to the C. P. R. construction in 1883; the V. & T. No. 5, named CARSON, became C. P. R. No. 4, the SAVONA, while the former V. & T. No. 7, the NEVADA, was assigned C. P. R. No. 5 and renamed the LYTTON. (Courtesy of H. L. Goldsmith)

local freight crew was shoving a cut of cars into a spur, the work being done on the fireman's side of the engine as the track curved in such a manner that the engineer could not see ahead. This fireboy was a student and when he suddenly called out, "Hold her!" the old engineer slowly applied his engine brake and said, "Now, son, when the brakemen give you a stop signal, you should say 'That will do' or 'That is good.' Never say 'Hold her' unless it is an emergency."

"Well, I don't know if this is an emergency or not," the fireman replied. "But we have shoved three cars over the end of the spur and them brakies are all giving wash-outs like mad down there!"

The majority of railroaders sympathized with the students and did their best to instruct them in the

safest methods of doing their work. Some students were adept at learning the numerous things required of them, while others struggled along until harsh experience taught them the lessons that made good hands out of them.

The average old-time railroader took great pride in his craft and would often do battle when he felt an official criticised him unjustly.

Along in the 1880's, Conductor Cy Bennett and his crew had halted their Oregon Pacific train at Corvallis and trooped into a restaurant for their noon meal. While dining, they were interrupted by the intrusion of the roadmaster, who began to berate the skipper over the loss of a hand car that had fallen off a car loaded with company material en route from Yaquina to Albany. Bennett shoved his plate aside, leaped to his feet and tossed the obnoxious brass hat through a window onto the sidewalk, then resumed his seat and finished his meal. Bennett's ready wit and quick temper once cost him his job as conductor on a narrow gauge pike in the Northwest. A baggage car in his mixed train caught fire and was destroyed despite the heroic efforts of the crew; the body of the car was consumed by flames, leaving only the trucks, which the crew rolled into a siding. The superintendent was waiting for Cy when the train reached the terminal, having been apprised of the conflagration by telegraph. The Old Man greeted the skipper sourly and in acid tones inquired what the conductor managed to save of the car. "The number and the running gear!" replied Bennett, and the Old Man fired him on the spot for being insubordinate.

An engineer on a branch line local had better luck. His road was conducting an extensive fuel-saving campaign shortly after they had converted their power from wood to oil. The runner's regular engine broke down one day and a locomotive of a larger type was substituted. A few days later the engineer received a curt letter demanding the reason for using more fuel oil on the trip with the larger locomotive while handling his usual consist. Moistening his stub of a pencil, the engineer scrawled this classic reply: "For the same reason that an elephant, pulling a baby buggy, will eat more hay than a billy goat."

In the wild and careless days of early railroading the crews were pretty much a law unto themselves, going about their work unmolested by officials if they got their trains over the road without losing too much time or breaking up the equipment. This atmosphere of independence led to conditions that soon came to a head and resulted in stricter regulations and increased supervision. Rule G, forbidding the use of alcohol, was openly winked at on some roads until the excess use of bottled spirits caused costly accidents. On one road in the Northwest, Sundays were observed by the non-operation of trains, but the crews usually gathered at the roundhouse to tinker with their pet engines. In warm weather these Sunday repair and bull sessions were enlivened by a keg of beer paid for by contributions from the crews, and a photo is in existence showing the boys grouped around one of these convivial kegs; prominently hoisting a foamy schooner in the foreground of this photo is the portly old Master Mechanic. Such camaraderie and sociable elbow-bending would give present-day officials mild cases of the horrors, but it helped maintain pleasant relations between brass hats and the crews of other years and

CANADIAN PACIFIC RAILWAY No. 6, the NICOLA, is shown here at Keefer, British Columbia, in 1885. Her tender is apparently a homemade affair, fabricated from a flat car with a wooden water tank at the rear and a panel fence forward to hold her fuel wood. An American type, Baldwin Shop No. 7273, she was built for the Onderdonk contract work in 1884, had 63 inch drivers and 16x24 inch cylinders. In 1887 she became Intercolonial Railway No. 184, later Canadian National Railways No. 236, and was cut up in 1925. Her name was likely derived from Nicola Lake and Nicola Camp in the mining district south of Kamloops and east of Lytton. (Courtesy of H. L. Goldsmith)

was a part of the esprit de corps that kept labor troubles at a minimum.

The untrammeled authority of conductors on early Western roads led to one black mark on the escutcheon of railroaders. Much of the local passenger traffic was conducted on the cash fare basis and a few skippers fell into the habit of pocketing this revenue and neglecting to turn it over to the companies at the end of their runs. The disease spread and was making severe dents in the receipts until the officials resorted to planting spotters aboard the trains and firing the offenders. Conductors who were guilty of stealing cash fares were called "color blind" by the rest of the clan, meaning that the looter could not differentiate the color of the company's money from his own. One of these "color blind" skippers is reputed to have entered the baggage car, tossed a wad of currency into the air, and remarked, "All that balances on the bell cord belongs to the Company!" while another tempered his petty larceny by spreading the cash fares on a trunk and dividing them into two piles, using the counting system of "two for us, one for the Company." This evil was not always the result of sheer dishonesty. One narrow gauge line in the throes of bankruptcy and receivership was so destitute that wages fell six months or more in arrears, and the conductors began to withhold the cash fares and distribute them to the employees to enable them to feed and clothe their families.

Some conductors developed an uncanny ability to detect the presence of a spotter and devised numer-

VICTORIA & SIDNEY RAILROAD, operating on British Columbia's Vancouver Island, used wood for fuel on the grates of Engine No. 3, a 4-4-0 with sunflower stack, shown here with a coach from the Esquimalt & Naniamo in the background. The engine displays a link in the slot of her Janney coupler knuckle, a device that made it possible to couple interchangeably with link and pin or automatic coupler equipment. (Courtesy of El White)

CANADIAN COLLIERYS (DUNSMUIR) LTD., operated pioneer coal mining projects on Vancouver Island, British Columbia, and narrow gauge rails served to transport the produce of the mines. Pictured here is the DUKE, one of the neat little saddle tanks engaged in hauling coal. An 0-6-0 with a diamond stack, the DUKE went to the scrappers in 1909. An 0-4-0 named the PIONEER and built in Staleybridge, England, in 1863 and operated by the Vancouver Coal Company is reputed to have been the first locomotive to operate in British Columbia. This little engine, weighing 10 tons, featured a typical open English cab with "spectacle plate" that likely did not endear her to the engineer in the rainy winter season. (Courtesy of El White)

tion days, as well as pitched battles between the crews of rival railroads when one road attempted to cross another.

Train robbers added their measure of excitement to the job of railroading when the trains took over the rich express shipments formerly carried by stage coach or river steamer.

The robbery of the northbound *Oregon Express* of the Southern Pacific Lines in 1897 followed a standard pattern favored by train robbers. Engineer Dick Morris was at the throttle of the passenger train as it neared Roseburg at approximately 11:30 P. M. on the night of January 28th. He was flagged down by a man just as his engine emerged from a rock cut near Shady Point. The flagman called him to the gangway where the startled runner was covered by an armed man who had evidently hidden on the tank of the locomotive. Fireman Hendricks witnessed this action and leaped from his cab window, the bandits firing several shots in his direction as he plunged down the embankment in the dark. Making good his escape, Hendricks followed along the banks of the South Umpqua River until out of range, then struck off along the tracks toward Roseburg to secure help. The two robbers blew open the door of the express car when Messenger Butler refused to open it, entered, and covered the stunned messenger. They then calmly proceeded to blow open the safe and looted it of a sizable sum of money, making their escape into the dark winter night. They were never apprehended, although the railroad detectives pursued a number of clues. Fate played a part in aiding them to escape. A farmer living near the scene heard the shots fired at Fireman Hendricks, followed by the explosion when the express car was blown open. He surmised that a robbery was in progress and started across his field toward the

ous methods to outwit them, but the looting of cash fares was eventually stamped out.

Rail lines began to serve the region west of the Rockies when law and order were still in their infancy, and pioneer railroaders often rubbed elbows with frontier violence. When the Oregonian Railway was extending its narrow gauge trackage across the floor of the Willamette Valley, a spike driver named Searles got into a brawl with a number of Mongolian laborers over a bucket of drinking water. The Orientals ganged up on the white man, but he swung his spike maul with such accuracy that one of his attackers suffered a broken arm and another received a blow on the head that sent him to join his ancestors. The enraged mob, fired by the death of their member, renewed their assault with such violence that Searles retreated to the work train locomotive and the engine crew hastily got under way, wheeling the fugitive out of reach. The Orientals then turned on the white foreman who had been left behind by the trainmen in their dash for safety. The foreman calmly hauled out a six-shooter and, in the words of a newspaper scribe who recorded the event, "sent them skulking down the grade like a pack of coyotes."

There were other recorded instances of violence in dealing with the Chinese labor gangs in construc-

train, armed with his trusty rifle. Before he reached the scene, he noted the flames mounting from the express car, which had caught fire from the explosion of the robbers' bomb, and decided that the train had been wrecked and was burning. He rushed back to his house and exchanged his rifle for an axe and a water bucket, then hurried back to fight the fire. As he ran across the flame-lit meadow, he passed within speaking distance of the two bandits fleeing with their sack of stolen money!

A Northern Pacific engineer was held up at Mullan, Idaho, in 1899, but in this case the motive was not train robbery. Engineer L. W. Hutton was captured by a mob of striking miners and was forced at gunpoint to halt his train at a powder house while the mob loaded up kegs of explosives. Then, still covered by the weapons of the strikers, Hutton was forced to leave the Northern Pacific tracks and run over the rails of the Coeur d'Alene Railway & Navigation Co. to Wallace, Idaho, where the mob blew up the plant of the big Bunker Hill mine. The trip over the Coeur d'Alene line, running without orders and expecting to meet a train of that road at every curve, caused the engineer more worry than the black muzzles of the guns the strikers kept pointed at his head.

Fast runs, along with forced runs, added spice to early-day railroading. Crews wheeled their engines at excessive speeds for a variety of reasons. Some mad dashes were made hauling equipment to combat fires that raged through the flimsy wooden structures of infant cities, while other speedy runs were made in attempts to capture mail contracts from rival roads. When flames threatened to destroy Portland in 1872, Engineer Joe Callicott wheeled an Oregon & California relief train loaded with Salem's fire equipment to the conflagration. Although the track was new and not thoroughly settled, he put his woodburning eight-wheeler over it at a gait not equaled for many years and comparable to the schedule of the crack streamliners operating over the improved roadbed of today.

One of the fascinating aspects of railroading was the constant variety of traffic flowing over the iron highway. When General Edward R. S. Canby was murdered by Indians during the Modoc War in 1873, his remains were carried from the end of the Oregon & California tracks at Roseburg to Portland by a special funeral train. The steam cars moved troops in war time, and deposited thousands of gold hunters in Seattle for the rush to the Yukon in 1898. Presidents and celebrities toured the region by rail, and the iron horse brought the colorful railroad circus to hinterland villages. In 1888 the New York Museum sent a "Menagerie Car" through the Northwest, complete with steam calliope and a wondrous exhibit of rare living animals, snakes, and brilliant-plumaged tropical birds.

The famous Sells Circus toured the Northwest in 1891 and set the stage for a railroad anecdote long remembered by the crew involved. The show was moving into California over the Southern Pacific and one of the cars in the train carried Jumbo, Jr., the elephant that was a star performer with the troupe. Above Delta station, this playful pachyderm managed to get his trunk through an opening in

PUGET SOUND PIONEER, this little 4-4-0 was named the ALKI and was No. 2 on the narrow gauge roster of the Columbia & Puget Sound Railroad. She was a product of the National Locomotive Works, Connellsville, Pennsylvania, and is shown here on the gallows style turntable at the Seattle roundhouse. The railroad water tank and the wharf bordering Puget Sound can be seen in the background. (Courtesy of C. W. Mendenhall)

COLUMBIA & PUGET SOUND RAILROAD'S No. 9 was a sturdy narrow gauge Consolidation type, a product of the Grant Locomotive Works. The road, which later became the Pacific Coast Railroad, handled heavy coal drags from the mines along the route. The main stem extended from Seattle to Franklin, Washington, with branches from Renton to Talbot and Coal Creek and additional branches serving Bruce, Kummer, and Taylor. Engine 9 later had her diamond stack replaced by a straight capped stack. (Courtesy of Joe Williamson, Marine Photo Shop)

the end of his car and extracted the coupling pin from the draw-head. The track along the Sacramento River canyon in the region is crooked and winding, so the engine crew clattered merrily along, blissfully unaware that their train had parted. The forward portion travelled nearly twenty miles before it was discovered that the elephant car and the rear portion of the circus train had been left stranded in the rugged mountains.

Rivalling the colorful circus trains was the special bearing Dr. W. S. Webb and party on a tour of the Pacific Northwest in the spring of 1889. Dr. Webb married the daughter of old W. H. Vanderbilt and, in a party numbering eleven, made the grand tour of the Golden West. A reporter of the day noted that "all (of the party) are worth untold wealth, and the four special cars are veritable palaces on wheels." Drawn by polished engines manned by select crews, the Webb party leisurely viewed the rough and uncouth West from the palatial splendor of their private chariots, gazing in awe at the majestic scenery while the natives stared in amazement at the display of luxury.

The true stories of adventure, fast runs, wrecks, and unusual happenings on the rail lines in the Northwest would fill a good many books, with some of the incidents stretching the credulity of the reader. But let us leave the land of majestic mountains, rushing streams, and endless forests for a moment, and, turning back the pages of Time, look in on a festive evening with a jolly crowd of stout-hearted Britishers.

In April, 1880, a group of officials and employees sat down to a testimonial dinner at the Crown Hotel, Stamford, England. Guest of honor for the eve-

ning was William Lightfoot, a locomotive driver retiring after 31 years of service on England's Great Northern Railway. The keen-eyed old gentleman with the bushy white beard listened to the toasts and speeches with quiet pride, and upon presentation of a fine marble clock, complete with engraved silver plaque, he arose and made a brief response. His railroad career had started in 1832 as an engine driver but he had previously worked for George Stephenson during construction of the pioneer locomotives. He had handled the regulator on Stephenson's primitive engines and drove Robert Stephenson's *Rocket*, made famous at the Rainhill trials. In 1835 he was the driver of a locomotive that exploded at Millsbury, Yorkshire. Mr. Lightfoot left the Stockton & Darlington road in 1838 and drove the first engine on the London-Birmingham line. After 7 years of service there, he was engaged to go to France as a driver on the Orleans and Bordeaux line, returning to England in 1856 as a driver at Stamford. Lord Exeter appointed him locomotive foreman when the Sibson line was opened, a position he held for 7 years. He had operated the train taking the Duc de Montspencier from France to Spain, and on several occasions had been the driver of the train carrying Her Majesty, the Queen of England. However, rank nor station influenced him not, his desire being to handle his train safely, regardless of the haughty or humble character of his passengers. Now, after 2,000,000 miles of engine driving and many narrow escapes, he was retiring and hoped to live long to enjoy the many friendships made in his long career on the foot-plate. His response was followed by cheers and applause, plus a number of toasts. The *Stamford and Ruthland*

Guardian remarked that "Wines and grog were put upon the table without stint."

But this is more than a recital of the adventures of a British engine driver, for William Lightfoot started a tradition that he likely never dreamed would see the wheel come a full turn. In 1873 he paid a $300 fee to have his son, James, entered as an apprentice machinist on the London, Brighton & South Coast Railway, a line whose locomotives were under the supervision of the noted William Stroudley. James Lightfoot served his 7-year apprenticeship without pay and became a skilled machinist. In 1891 he came to Canada as foreman of the Canadian Pacific Railway backshops in Winnipeg and served faithfully for many years.

James Lightfoot's son, William, was named for his paternal ancestor, and this lad grew up steeped in the railway tradition. Young William returned to England and hired out as a wiper on the London & South Western Railway in 1898, returning to Canada in 1899 to take a job on the Canadian Pacific. He was set out firing in 1901 and promoted to locomotive engineer in 1904, running out of Kenora when that terminal was called Rat Portage. In 1907 he left the C. P. R. and came to the United States, hiring out as an engineer on the Great Northern Railway at Spokane, Washington. Leaving the Hill road in 1910, he came to Oregon and hired out as an engineer on the Southern Pacific. William Lightfoot remained on the Portland Division until his retirement in 1947. Even then the name did not vanish from the roster of enginemen, for his son, William P. Lightfoot, followed in his father's footsteps on the same road. The boy began his rail service as a roundhouse laborer in 1936, went firing in 1941, and was promoted to engineer in 1946. Running out of Eugene, Oregon, young Bill handled the throttle on the huge S. P. cab-in-front type Articulated Consolidations. The pioneer *Rocket* and the *Puffing Billy* operated by his great-grandfather were watch-fob miniatures compared to these big mountain climbers, but the basic principles were unchanged. The canvas and red lead steam joints of the first William Lightfoot's day were scarcely a memory, but fire and water still produced the steam that urged the modern behemoths up the Cascade grades.

In the 1950's, the last of the giant steam engines were replaced by the invention of Dr. Rudolph Diesel and the life cycle of the steam locomotive was completed. Here in the evergreen empire of the Pacific Northwest the fourth generation of the Lightfoot clan witnessed the passing of a machine that was born under the hands of his ancestor and the remarkable saga of steam on the rails reached its conclusion.

COLUMBIA & PUGET SOUND RAILROAD, operated by the Pacific Coast Company, transported coal from the mines to the bunkers located in Seattle, Washington. Originally a narrow gauge and first operated as the Seattle & Walla Walla Railroad, the line was standardized in later years. Narrow gauge yard engine No. 5, an 0-6-0, did the chores around the Seattle yards. Note the metal-shod pole on the running board, used for staking cars by in switching movements. The locomotive is innocent of brake equipment, stops being made by the application of the hand brake on the tender by the fireman; in case of emergency, the runner could reverse the engine and give her a shot of steam. (Courtesy of Joe Williamson, Marine Photo Shop)

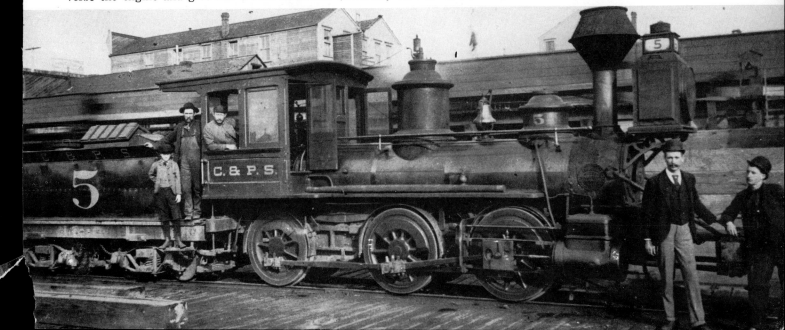

CANADIAN PACIFIC RAILWAY No. 8, named the SHUSHWAP, as she appeared at Yale, British Columbia, in 1885. The 4-4-0 was a Baldwin of 1884, bearing builder's number 7498. She had 16 x 24 inch cylinders and 51 inch drivers. In 1887 the SHUSHWAP became Intercolonial Railway No. 186, renumbered 1079 in 1912. In 1915 she was sold to Kirk & Cook, contractors engaged in building the Saint John Valley Railway. (Courtesy of H. L. Goldsmith)

CANADIAN PACIFIC RAILWAY No. 9, named the COLUMBIA, was a Baldwin 4-4-0, outshopped in 1884 with shop number 7501 on her builder's plate. She was the last of nine locomotives used on the Onderdonk contracts and is shown here at Keefer, British Columbia, in 1885. (Courtesy of H. L. Goldsmith)

BELLINGHAM BAY & BRITISH COLUMBIA RAILROAD ran from New Whatcom, Washington, to a junction with the Canadian Pacific at the border town of Sumas, with a branch to Lynden and an extension into the region drained by the south fork of the Nooksack River terminating at Glacier. Engine No. 3, shown here at Sumas in 1898, was a 4-4-0 built by Baldwin in 1891, Shop No. 11517. She had 17 x 24 inch cylinders, 62 inch drivers, and was noted for her speed. Originally burning wood, the engine was converted to coal and later to fuel oil. She was wrecked in a runaway down the steep grade of a logging line near Acme, Washington, killing Engineer Jack Treutle; formerly a runner on the B. & O. S. W., Treutle had been the engineer on her when she first went into service on the Bellingham Bay & British Columbia. (Courtesy of Fred Jukes)

PERHAPS A SHAPELY ANKLE is the attraction causing the brakie and the fireboy to neglect their duties as old No. 5 rolls away from the Bellingham depot in this fine action shot taken by Fred Jukes in 1906. The 2-8-0 was purchased by the Bellingham Bay & British Columbia from the Hicks Locomotive & Car Works, dealers in used railway equipment, and is reputed to have been the former No. 231 of the Union Pacific, later renumbered 1265 before going to the Hicks firm for re-sale. Built by Baldwin in 1881, Shop No. 5943, the hog had 19 x 24 inch cylinders and 50 inch drivers. The B. B. & B. C. purchased her in 1900 and used her on log trains, later utilizing her on the Lynden local; for many years her regular engineer was William Storey. (Courtesy of Fred Jukes)

BALDWIN MOGUL TYPE, No. 4 of the Bellingham Bay & British Columbia Railroad was built in 1891, Shop No. 12231, and was equally at home on freight or passenger runs. She had 17 x 24 inch cylinders, 54 inch drivers, and an extended wagon top boiler. Originally using wood for fuel, she had been converted to coal when Fred Jukes recorded her appearance in 1908. Under Bellingham & Northern operations old No. 4 lost her crown sheet at Sumas, killing her fireman. (Courtesy of Fred Jukes)

THE CAMERA OF FRED JUKES captured this likeness of No. 7 of the Bellingham Bay & British Columbia in 1908. The 4-6-0 was purchased from Hicks Locomotive & Car Works in 1902 by the Bellingham Bay & Eastern Railroad for use in construction of the Silver Beach-Wickersham line, and upon completion she was sold to the Bellingham Bay & British Columbia. There is some dispute as to where this engine came from, with factions claiming Pennsylvania Railroad and Union Pacific ancestry; whatever her origin, she earned the reputation of being a hard steamer. (Courtesy of Fred Jukes)

SEATTLE WATERFRONT SCENE shows narrow gauge Engine 10 of the Columbia & Puget Sound Railroad, backed by link and pin coal cars on the trestle in the background. The small boy in knee pants helps the fireman and engineer pose for this view of the little Baldwin 4-4-0. Most of the narrow gauge power from this road reportedly was shipped north to the White Pass & Yukon Railway. No record exists regarding the final disposition of the Columbia & Puget Sound's No. 1, a Mason 0-6-4 named the A. A. DENNY, but Fred Jukes reports a boiler, with a center casting, in use as a stationary power plant at the shops in Seattle many years ago and this is a clue to the possible fate of C. & P. S. Engine 1. (Courtesy of Joe Williamson, Marine Photo Shop)

EASTBOUND TRANSCONTINENTAL, Canadian Pacific Railway's Engine 47 and a 4-car passenger consist halts at Donald, British Columbia, in the 1890's. Ahead lies Ottertail, Field, and the crest of the Rocky Mountains; to the rear, the ribbons of steel pass Beaver Mouth, Revelstoke, and Kamloops, then thread the rugged gorge of the Fraser down to tidewater at Port Moody and Vancouver. Engine 47 was a 4-4-0 built by the Pittsburgh Locomotive Works in 1882, Shop No. 552. She had 17 x 24 inch cylinders and 58 inch drivers, ending her days in 1902, when she was scrapped. (Courtesy of Canadian Pacific Railway)

NORTHERN PACIFIC'S No. 220, photographed at Missoula, Montana, in 1884, was a sturdy 4-4-0 built by the Portland Locomotive Works in Portland, Maine. The engine, bearing construction number 459, left the factory in 1883. In 1897 the Northern Pacific renumbered her 896. The early locomotives of the N. P. burned wood when the line was pushed through the Northwest, but coal later replaced the pungent fir and pine as fuel for the hungry fireboxes. (Courtesy of Ronald V. Nixon)

SEATTLE LAKE SHORE & EASTERN RAILWAY, a standard gauge road later acquired by the Northern Pacific, was the proud possessor of this Rhode Island 2-8-0, assigned road number 7 and named the S. V. WHITE. The road operated coal bunkers and an ocean dock in Smith's Cove on Elliott Bay in Seattle, with the main line extending east to Woodinville, where it divided; the north fork went to Snohomish and the east fork to Snoqualmie. Mud guards cover old No. 7's drivers, but the hazardous dash along the running board by her fireman for the purpose of filling her tallow cups has been eliminated by the application of lubrication pipes fed from her cab. (Courtesy of Charles E. Fisher)

SHELTON SOUTHWESTERN RAILROAD lived up to its corporate title, running southwesterly out of Shelton, Washington. Shelton, on an arm of Puget Sound known as "Big Skookum", was the terminus for extensive logging railroad operations. The Shelton Southwestern's No. 2, shown here, was a woodburning 2-6-0; the line served a richly timbered region and logs formed the major portion of the traffic. (Courtesy of C. W. Mendenhall)

SEATTLE & NORTHERN RAILWAY operated from Anacortes to Rockport, Washington, a distance of about 54 miles. The line served the island-studded region where the Straits of Juan de Fuca merge with the inland seas of Puget Sound. In 1902 the road was absorbed by the Seattle & Montana Railroad, a Great Northern subsidiary connecting Seattle with New Westminster, British Columbia. Engine No. 2 of the Seattle & Northern, shown here with a 4-wheel caboose of the Columbia & Puget Sound, was a 4-4-0 built by the New York Locomotive Works in 1890; she had 62 inch drivers, 17x24 inch cylinders, and carried 140 pounds of steam pressure. Courtesy of C. W. Mendenhall)

PUGET SOUND SHUNTER, this clean 0-6-0 was Northern Pacific's No. 137, taken at Tacoma, Washington, in 1896. She was a Baldwin, Shop No. 6427, built in 1882; in 1898 the N.P. renumbered her 970. Fireman M. B. Morrow, dressed in white and standing in front of the air pump, was later a Northern Pacific fuel inspector, now retired and living in Montana; although in his eighties, he is still spry and active. Mr. Morrow was the inventor of the Cyclone Spark Arrestor, a locomotive device widely used both here and abroad. (Courtesy of Ronald V. Nixon)

HEAVY DUTY HOG, old No. 485 of the Northern Pacific is shown at Helena, Montana, in 1889, the year she left the Baldwin Locomotive Works with construction number 10441 on her builder's plate. Renumbered N. P. 58 in 1898, she and her sister engines of this type rendered many years of faithful service on the western lines, some remaining in active operation into the 1940's. Engineer George Howe is shown in this photo which belonged to Trainmaster J. R. Smith, taken when the 485 was equipped with link and pin coupler, wooden cab, and stave pilot. (Courtesy of Ronald V. Nixon)

ELKHORN, MONTANA provided the setting for this view of Northern Pacific's No. 149 in the year 1894. Baldwin's No. 6629, the Mogul type was built in 1883 and later was renumbered 599 by the N. P.; she was scrapped in Livingston, Montana, in September, 1915. The Elkhorn Branch extended from Boulder to Elkhorn, slightly over 20 miles, and is now abandoned. (Courtesy of Ronald V. Nixon)

NORTHERN PACIFIC No. 676 is backed by an unusual water tank in this photo taken at Missoula in 1903. The 4-4-0 was formerly No. 2 on the Montana Union Railroad, and was built by the New York Loco. Works of Rome, New York, in 1887, builders number 250. The man at the left is Charles Dickman, now retired. The diagonal lettering on the box car in the right background reads, "Air Brake Merchandise". (Courtesy of Ronald V. Nixon)

PUGET SOUND & GRAY'S HARBOR RAILROAD ran from New Kamilchie to Matlock, Washington, serving Summit, Buck's Prairie, and the Cloquallum Creek region. The line was owned by Captain William Renton, who had opened the Port Blakely sawmill in 1853, and was known as the "Blakely Road." Construction on this logging pike was started in 1887 under the direction of Sol G. Simpson; Simpson founded the Simpson Logging Company in 1895 and this concern still is in operation, its logging road powered by steam locomotives until they were recently replaced by Diesels. This photo shows Puget Sound & Gray's Harbor No. 7, a Baldwin 2-4-2 saddle tank. (Courtesy of C. W. Mendenhall)

TAKING FIVE, the gang at Siskiyou station gaze into the camera lens for the photographer who exposed this plate about 1887. Located on the lofty summit of the Siskiyou Mountains, this station was the temporary terminus of the Southern Pacific tracks reaching north from Dunsmuir toward Ashland, Oregon. The six-horse stage coach at the platform furnished connections from this railhead to the end of track of the Oregon & California Railroad, building south from Ashland. The engine in the foreground holds a string of varnished cars while the blurred locomotive at the right steams away from the turntable. In later years, the tunnel located near this station was the site of the notorious D'Autremont brothers' attempt to rob a Southern Pacific passenger train, resulting in the cold-blooded murder of an engineer, fireman, brakeman, and express messenger. The three D'Autremont brothers never obtained any loot from the hold-up, were later captured, and all sentenced to life in prison. (Courtesy of Southern Pacific)

SPOKANE & PALOUSE started life as the Eastern Washington Railway Company, incorporated by Northern Pacific interests in 1885. The name was changed to Spokane & Palouse in 1886 and 103.66 miles of track were constructed by 1888, running from Marshall, Washington, to Genesee, Idaho. A branch from Belmont to Farmington Junction, 6 miles, was completed in 1890, and a 40-mile line from Pullman Junction to Julia-etta, Idaho, was placed in service around 1891. The line was operated by the Northern Pacific, and was sold to them in 1899. This photo shows Spokane & Palouse No. 3, an American Standard, with a 4th of July excursion train in 1887. (Courtesy of Ronald V. Nixon)

PENINSULAR RAILWAY COMPANY operated No. 6, a woodburning 2-6-2 built by Baldwin, on log trains running through the Washington forests at the base of the Olympic Peninsula. The road ran from Shelton to Gordonville, the latter terminus being located in Washington's Humptulips country near the briny waters of the Pacific Ocean. Note the two link and pin drawheads on this engine; the lower one may have been used for skidding logs. The fact that the Pacific Northwest was a part of the legendary Paul Bunyan's domain may have accounted for the king-sized long oiler held by the 6-Spot's hogger. (Courtesy of C. W. Mendenhall)

IDAHO & WASHINGTON NORTHERN was incorporated in 1907 and built a standard gauge line 43.1 miles long to Newport, Washington. This line was extended 50.6 miles in 1910 to Ione, and in 1911 another 9.5 miles were added, bringing the rails into Metaline Falls, Washington. A branch built in 1907 ran 6.54 miles between Clagstone Junction and Coleman, Idaho. The road was acquired, through a foreclosure sale by the Chicago, Milwaukee & St. Paul in 1916. Shown here is Idaho & Washington Northern's 4-6-0 type, No. 17, with a passenger train at Usk, Washington, in 1912. This engine later became the Milwaukee's No. 2717. (Courtesy of Ronald V. Nixon)

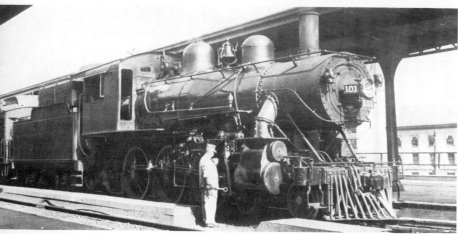

SPOKANE INTERNATIONAL RAILROAD built a standard gauge line 152 miles long from Spokane, Washington, to the Canadian border at Eastport, Idaho, not long after the turn of the century. Engine No. 1 was a 4-6-0 built new for the road by Rogers in May, 1907, bearing builders number 42948. This locomotive was rebuilt around 1920, with the addition of a superheater and piston valves. Renumbered the 101, this photo shows her heading up a passenger train at the Spokane depot. (Courtesy of Ronald V. Nixon)

BUTTE, ANACONDA & PACIFIC No. 18 at Anaconda, Montana, in 1899. This bulky 4-8-0 was built by Schenectady to handle the heavy drags of copper ore from the mines at Butte to the big smelter located at Anaconda. The 25-mile line is still in operation. (Courtesy of Ronald V. Nixon)

OREGON RAILWAY & NAVIGATION COMPANY started life as the Oregon Steam Navigation Company, a steamboat operation on the Columbia River and tributaries in northern Oregon. Rail service was instituted to portage passengers and freight around the rapids, rocks, and falls in the Columbia at the Cascades and Celilo. These two portage lines formed a part of the main line built from Portland to a connection with the Northern Pacific at Wallula, a project of Henry Villard that gave Portland it's first transcontinental rail connection. Engine 73, shown here with pilot bar coupler and single stage compressor at Albina roundhouse, was a Baldwin 4-4-0 of 1883 vintage, originally O. R. & N. 81; under Union Pacific control in the 1890's, she was numbered Union Pacific 549, later becoming Oregon Railroad & Navigation No. 73, then Union Pacific No. 1108. (Courtesy of Fred Jukes)

GILMORE & PITTSBURG RAIL-ROAD operated from Armstead, in southwestern Montana, to Leadore and Salmon, Idaho, through some-exceptionally rugged terrain. This photo at Armstead in 1904 shows the first passenger train over the now-abandoned road, headed by Engine 11, a sturdy 2-8-2 built by Baldwin. Courtesy of Ronald V. Nixon).

ON THE PLAINS OF MONTANA during construction days the bearded crew, two small boys, and a dog all gather around Great Northern's Engine 152 to have their picture taken. The light rails are laid on hewn ties and the roadbed is innocent of ballast, but the route of the Empire Builder was stretching toward the salt chuck on the Pacific Ocean. Note the ash pan hoe carried on the tank trucks. (Courtesy of Ben W. Griffiths)

BUTTE, ANACONDA & PACIFIC RAILWAY was chartered as a standard gauge road in 1892 and opened in 1894 to connect the copper mines at Butte with the reduction works at Anaconda, Montana. The road was controlled by the Anaconda Copper Mining Company, which also leased the Montana Railway from Stuart to Anaconda. This photo was presented to R. V. Nixon by Fireman Wilkins, the man with his hand on the steam chest. Taken at Anaconda in 1900, it shows B. A. & P. Engine 50 on the regular Butte-Anaconda passenger train with the locomotive festooned with black crepe, mourning the death of Marcus Daley, the famed Montana "Copper King". (Courtesy of Ronald V. Nixon)

MONTANA RAILROAD was a standard gauge line chartered in 1894. The first 56 miles of track, from Lombard to Leadboro, Montana, was opened for service in 1897; the extension from Summit to Harlowtown, 44 miles, was opened in 1900. A later extension, 63 miles long, carried the line into Lewistown. Absorbed by the Chicago, Milwaukee, St. Paul & Pacific a part of the old road now forms a section of the Milwaukee's main line. Montana Railroad's No. 5, shown here about 1908, was a 4-6-0 with odd counterbalances. (Courtesy of Ronald V. Nixon)

MASON COUNTY CENTRAL RAILROAD served the logging camps in the southern section of Washington's Olympic Peninsula. The road was organized about 1888 and operated out of the booming mill town of Shelton, located on Hammersley Inlet. Mason County Central's 4-Spot was this diamond stack 2-6-2, a rather uncommon wheel arrangement as the Prairie type was never very popular in the Northwest. (Courtesy of C. W. Mendenhall)

IDAHO CENTRAL RAILROAD, incorporated in 1886, planned a grandiose enterprise that included a rail line from Nampa, Idaho, to Yaquina Bay, Oregon, with an extension east to a junction with the Northern Pacific, the latter line to pass through Boise. Actually, only 20 miles of track were built, linking Nampa with Boise, and the line was later absorbed into the Oregon Short Line system. This photo shows Idaho Central's No. 1, a 4-4-0, with the first train to arrive in Boise; the date was September 5th, 1887. Residents of the Idaho capitol called this short line "The Stub." (Courtesy of Henry R. Griffiths, Jr.)

ALBINA, OREGON, ROUNDHOUSE furnished the setting for this view of Union Pacific Railroad's No. 549, originally the 81 of the Oregon Railway & Navigation Company. Albina was a separate municipality on the eastern shore of the Willamette River opposite Portland, consolidated with the latter city in 1891. Headquarters and terminus of the O. R. & N. were located in Albina, with ferry service across the river to Portland, and during the turbulent years of railroad activity from 1872 through the 1890's, the town achieved a reputation for rough and tough doings. Terminal facilities of the Union Pacific are still centered at the old Albina location. (Courtesy of Arthur M. Sayre)

SILVER STATE MOGUL. From Nevada's Comstock Lode region came this Cooke-built 2-6-0 to serve in Oregon's Evergreen Empire. The engine was built in 1872 as No. 15 of the fabled Virginia & Truckee Railroad and named the AURORA. In 1881 she was purchased by the Oregon Railway & Navigation Company for $9,500 and renumbered O. R. & N. 39. Under the Union Pacific control in 1890-94, she bore the number 1380, then was renumbered O. R. & N. 17. Three other Virginia & Truckee 2-6-0's were acquired by the Oregon line in 1881, these being the COMSTOCK, the WASHOE, and the OPHIR. (Courtesy of J. E. Broyles)

MAGNIFICENT PHOTOGRAPH of the Northern Pacific terminal at Missoula, Montana, was taken in 1883. The roundhouse here consisted of seven sheds arranged in a semi-circle facing the turntable. The five sheds from the right appear to contain two tracks each, providing 10 stalls, while the two buildings at the left probably contained shop equipment. Portions of nine woodburning locomotives are visible in this rare view. The tents and cabins in the foreground probably served as living quarters for railroad employees; the street at the far right is now Higgins Avenue, Missoula's main drag. (Courtesy of Ronald V. Nixon)

NORTHERN PACIFIC'S No. 420 and her crew as they appeared at the Missoula roundhouse in 1889. This 4-4-0 was of the heaviest class of American Standards on the N. P. system and was built by Baldwin, Shop No. 8683, in 1887. The engine was renumbered 667 in 1898. Beyond the tank of the locomotive can be seen the roundhouse that replaced the original wooden engine sheds used at Missoula. (Courtesy of Ronald V. Nixon)

ACROSS THE RIVER OF THE WEST, old No. 1 and her passenger train get a lift from a Columbia River train ferry. The 4-4-0 and her string of varnish belong to the Portland, Vancouver & Yakima Railway, a line that ran out of Portland, barged across the mighty Columbia to Vancouver, but never reached Yakima, Washington, the terminus indicated in its' name. The road got as far as Yacolt, in the region remembered for a terrible forest fire known as the "Yacolt Burn", and later passed into the hands of the Northern Pacific, reduced to the status of a branch. (Oregon Historical Society photo, courtesy of John T. Labbe)

ASTORIA & COLUMBIA RIVER RAILROAD provided the connecting link between Portland and Astoria, Oregon, with an extension from the port at the mouth of the Columbia on to the resort village of Seaside. The road was pushed to completion by A. B. Hammond, a powerful figure in Oregon's rail development. Engine No. 7 was built by Rogers in 1883, Shop No. 3411, as the 2-Spot of the Willamette Valley & Coast Railroad and operated between Albany and Yaquina. The road later became the Oregon Pacific Railroad, fathered by Colonel T. E. Hogg. In 1896, after the Hogg enterprise collapsed, the graceful American Standard was acquired by the Astoria & Columbia River, in later years becoming No. 54 of the Spokane, Portland & Seattle Railway when that road absorbed the Astoria line. (Willis Gulker collection, courtesy of Vernon Goe and J. T. Labbe)

OREGON WATER POWER & RAILWAY COMPANY operated an electric line from Portland to Estacada and Cazadero, on the upper reaches of the Clackamas River. Built shortly after the turn of the century, the road used several steam locomotives for construction purposes. One of these, a diamond stack 4-4-0 numbered 107, is shown here; although reported to be a former Oregon Railway & Navigation Company engine, her cab roof is identical with those of early Baldwin engines used on the Northern Pacific. (Courtesy of John T. Labbe)

STEAM PAVES THE WAY for the electric operations to follow on the Springwater Division of the Oregon Water Power & Railway line running from Portland to Cazadero. The 4-4-0 Baldwin shown here is O. W. P.'s No. 112, built originally as No. 34 of the Oregon Railway & Navigation Company. Note the skeleton track and the cordwood piled on the tender. (Courtesy of John T. Labbe)

STEAM AT WORK. The ingenuity of railroaders found other work for locomotives than moving trains. When the California & Oregon Railroad was being pushed north from Marysville, California, to a junction with the Oregon & California road at Ashland, the rough terrain presented some difficult construction problems. These four diamond stack locomotives were spurred out and pressed into service as a battery of stationary boilers. They furnished steam to operate the row of pumps in the foreground; in the rear, at far right, a hydraulic system utilizes the water supplied by the pumps to sluice out a path for the tracks. The location of this novel method of construction was probably in the canyon of the Sacramento River. (Courtesy of Southern Pacific)

OREGON RAILROAD & NAVIGATION COMPANY used Engine 164 in freight and helper service out of La-Grande, Oregon, around the turn of the century. The 2-8-0 was built by the New York Locomotive Works in 1888 as the Oregon Railway & Navigation Company's No. 86, one of a group of five engines of this type called the "Rome hogs." Under Union Pacific control, this Consolidation became Union Pacific's No. 1291, renumbered O. R. & N. 164, and in 1915 became Union Pacific's 704; she was retired in 1933. (Courtesy of Fred Jukes)

COEUR D'ALENE RAILWAY & NAVIGATION COMPANY photographs are practically non-existent and in over 20 years of collecting railroad pictures, this is the first one the writer has encountered. The decorated engine is No. 2 of the Coeur d'Alene Railway & Navigation Company, posed at Wallace, Idaho, on July 4th, 1889. The flat car behind the locomotive has been fitted out with plank seats and a roof of boughs for an Independence Day excursion. Promoted by D. C. Corbin, the 3 foot gauge pike started in 1886 and built from Old Mission to Wallace, Idaho, via Wardner, with a branch from Wallace to Burke. The region around Wallace and Burke was rich mining country, and the "Chippy Road" handled a heavy traffic of ore and concentrates. It was acquired by the Northern Pacific about 1888 and converted to standard gauge about 1897, most of the narrow gauge power going north to the Yukon in the gold rush of '98. (Courtesy of Ronald V. Nixon)

PAYETTE VALLEY RAILROAD, incorporated in 1906, built a standard gauge road from Payette to New Plymouth, Idaho, a distance of 11 miles. The construction, started in April of 1906, and completed late in August, left an 18-mile gap between New Plymouth and Emmett. In 1910, the Payette Valley Extension Railroad completed this segment into Emmett, and both roads were leased to the Oregon Short Line on July 1st, 1914. The Oregon Short Line acquired the lines by purchase on August 5th, 1914. This photo shows Payette Valley's No. 104, a 4-4-0, with a consist of two combines and two coaches in the yards at Emmett, Idaho. (Courtesy of Henry R. Griffiths, Jr.)

PACIFIC RAILWAY & NAVIGATION COMPANY constructed a standard gauge road from Hillsboro to Tillamook, Oregon, linking the lush coastal region around Tillamook Bay with the outside world through a connection with the Southern Pacific at Hillsboro. The line, incorporated in 1905 and completed in 1911, passed through a section of the Coast Range rich in timber, and soon came into the hands of the Southern Pacific, currently operated as the Tillamook Branch. This photo shows Pacific Ry. & Nav. Co. Engine 1 at the frame depot at Buxton, Oregon, in 1907; Engineer Chas. Follett is in the cab, Fireman Harry McLauchlan in the gangway, Conductor J. G. Griffiths seated on the apron, and Brakeman Chas. Bartlett stands by the main driver. The Baldwin 4-4-0 was built in 1880 as No. 33 of the Northern Pacific, later renumbered 839, and was acquired by the P. R. & N. in 1905. She was scrapped in 1916. The American type had 17x24 inch cylinders and 63 inch drivers. (Courtesy of Ben W. Griffiths)

THE BLACK CREPE OF MOURNING draped over Southern Pacific's No. 2031 was in memory of Edward H. Harriman, the engine being decorated at the time of Harriman's death in September, 1909. The ten-wheeler was engaged in work train service during the construction of the Pacific Railway & Navigation Company when this photo was taken, the location being west of Buxton, Oregon. The crew, left to right, includes Brakeman "Dutch" Neil, Conductor J. G. Griffiths, Engineer Harry McLauchlan ,and Fireman Chet Alexander. The engine was built by the Schenectady works in 1876 as No. 218 of the Central Pacific. (Courtesy of Ben W. Griffiths)

POPPING OFF, PACIFIC ENGINEERING COMPANY'S No. 1 raises a plume of steam from her safety valve against a backdrop of Oregon firs. The 4-4-0 wood burner was in construction work on the Pacific Railway & Navigation Company's line from Hillsboro to Tillamook when this picture was taken. In the cab window is Al Wagner, for many years an engineer on the Portland Division of the Southern Pacific. The man in the gangway, dressed in light clothing, is Jim Gray; he was later to meet his death when he jumped from a runaway train on the Carlton Consolidated Lumber Company's railroad.

OREGON RAILWAY COMPANY was a 3-foot gauge pike that succeeded the Dayton, Sheridan & Grand Ronde Railroad, a line built by farmers and local promoters in Yamhill County, Oregon, in 1878. The Oregon Railway was soon reorganized as the Oregonian Railway Company, Ltd., a concern financed with Scottish capital and headed by the Earl of Airlie. This is a builder's photograph of Engine No. 4, a Pittsburgh-built 2-6-0 named the BROWNSVILLE in honor of the Willamette Valley village located on the East Side Division of the road. She had 12 x 16 inch cylinders, 36 inch drivers, and weighed 37,300 pounds; her tender held 1,235 gallons of water and slightly less than two cords of wood. The Mogul became 2nd 1025 of the Southern Pacific when they acquired the narrow gauge, and in 1906 she was sold to the McKenzie Shipyard in Oakland, California. (Courtesy of Charles E. Fisher)

GAZING FROM THE OPEN WINDOWS, passengers enjoy the wild scenery as a Southern Pacific passenger engine blasts up the Siskiyou Mountains in Southern Oregon. The curved timber structure is the Dollarhide trestle, named in honor of Clay Dollarhide; he maintained a pioneer toll road over the mountains, with a toll-gate near his house, the roof of which can be seen to the left of the trestling. The brigade of cars rolling over the iron highway supplanted the rough and comfortless horsedrawn stages that choked with summer's dust and bogged in winter's mire. The railroad grade over this section was both steep and crooked, necessitating the use of helper engines. (Courtesy of Southern Pacific)

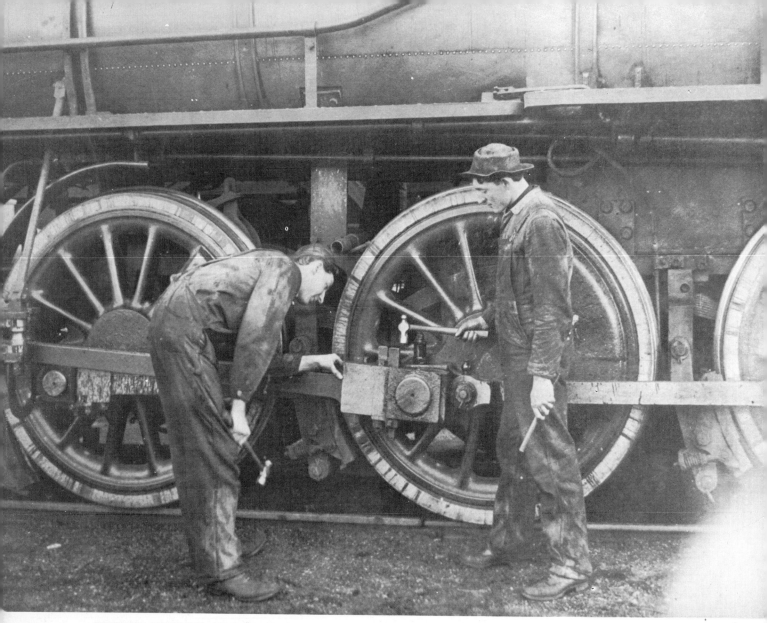

UNSUNG HEROES OF THE IRON HORSE'S STABLE, a machinist and his helper key up the crank pin brass in the back end of a main rod. Skilled in their trades, the mechanics, boiler makers, pipe fitters, and other shop personnel toiled in the murk and gloom of countless roundhouses to keep the locomotives in running order. The pair shown here, clothing smeared with grease and grime, are typical of the shop craft throughout the West and are at work on a 4-6-0 of the Southern Pacific in Roseburg, Oregon. (Lindsay collection, courtesy of Frank Erno)

COOS COAL HAULER, this quaint little 0-4-0 ran on the short line of the old Newport coal mine, later known as the Libby mine, near Marshfield, Oregon. Built by the National Iron Works of San Francisco, this engine bore the number 2, and could handle eight or nine small cars of coal from the mines down to the bunkers located on Isthmus Slough, a branch of Coos Bay. Here the black diamonds were loaded aboard ship, the bulk of the coal cargoes in the 1880's and 1890's going to the San Francisco market. (Courtesy of Jack Slattery, Jack's Photo Service)

ILWACO RAILWAY & NAVIGATION COMPANY, operating a 3-foot gauge line along the southwest Washington coastline, had passed into Union Pacific control when this photo was taken of Engine N1. The 4-4-0 was built by Baldwin in 1887 as No. 7 of the South Pacific Coast Railroad, where she was later renumbered 26. She was sold to the Ilwaco line in 1908 for $2,500 and became that road's second No. 3, later the N1 as shown here. She was scrapped in 1931. (Courtesy of Lamar Ferguson)

SALEM, FALLS CITY & WESTERN RAILWAY was chartered in 1901 to construct a standard gauge road from Salem, Oregon, to the Pacific Ocean. Promoted by L. and Geo. T. Gerlinger, the line was completed from Dallas to Falls City in 1903 and extended west to Black Rock in 1905, tapping an area rich in timber. The line from Dallas to West Salem was completed in 1909, but the road did not cross the Williamette River into Salem until early in 1913, about the time it came under Southern Pacific control. Engine No. 2, a woodburning 4-6-0, was reputedly built by Taunton in 1885 and acquired second-hand from the Oregon Railway & Navigation Company. The Gerlinger family, promoters of the road, also operated the Dallas Locomotive & Machine Works. Local wags dubbed the railroad the "Dutch Pacific".

CAR DEPARTMENT FORCE was responsible for repairing and inspecting railroad rolling stock, and the tapping of the car inspector's hammer as he tested equipment earned the craft the nicknames of car-tonks or car-whackers. The Union Pacific freight car shown here is away from home for the crew toiling over the forge and an arch bar truck are Southern Pacific employees at Roseburg, Oregon, in the early 1900's. (Lindsay collection, courtesy of Frank Erno)

SALT WATER SHUNTER, the 1-Spot of the Astoria & Columbia River Railroad was an 0-6-0 that did the switching chores around the historic port of Astoria. The town, an outgrowth of a fort and trading post founded by John Jacob Astor's men, was located on the south shore of the broad Columbia, much of the business district and warehouses being built on piling and wharves. This setup led to a disastrous fire in later years that nearly wiped out the city, but it was reconstructed and rail service is now provided by the Spokane, Portland & Seattle Railway, successor to Hammond's old Astoria & Columbia River. (Photo from the S. P. & S. "Dope Bucket", courtesy of J. T. Labbe)

THE PACIFIC NORTHWEST, with its numerous streams and plentiful supply of timber, was the home of a great many covered railroad bridge. This huge wooden truss with a 282½ foot span stretched across the crystal waters of the MacKenzie River between Coburg and Springfield, Oregon, on a Southern Pacific branch line; it was reputedly the longest single wooden span in existence when completed about 1890. Protected from the elements by the roof and siding, the stout wooden timbers of the truss lasted for many years and a number of these covered wooden railroad bridges still are in use in the western section of Oregon.

PACIFIC & IDAHO NORTHERN RAILWAY ran out of Weiser, Idaho, following the Weiser River along the eastern flank of the Seven Devils Mountains. The road built to Council, and by 1906, an extension of 41 miles was under way, headed toward Payette Lakes. This rare photo, taken at Diamond Springs tank near Midvale, shows No. 100, a diamond stack 4-6-0, on the mixed train in the foreground. Engine 101, another tenwheeler, is rounding the curve at the head end of a stock train. (Arthur Petersen collection, courtesy of H. R. Griffiths, Jr.)

WASHINGTON & COLUMBIA RIVER RAILWAY No. 1 at Hope, Idaho. This 4-6-0 was probably inherited from the Oregon & Washington Territory Railroad, known as the "Hunt Road" after its' builder, Geo. W. Hunt. The Washington & Columbia River Ry. was chartered July 30th, 1892, as a successor to the Hunt line, and was controlled by the Northern Pacific through bond ownership. When the line was later taken over by the Northern Pacific, this engine became N. P. No. 150, Class S-11. (Courtesy of Ronald V. Nixon)

THE ROUGH TERRAIN through which the western rail lines climbed necessitated many bridges and trestles, these flimsy structures being more economical than costly fills made with dump carts and manual labor. In later years, following the advent of heavier trains and improved earth-moving equipment, most of these early wooden trestles were replaced with fills. This photo shows three woodburning locomotives boosting a passenger train over White Point trestle, a noted landmark on the Southern Pacific's original route over the Siskiyou Mountains that formed a natural barrier between Oregon and California. (Courtsy of H. H. Arey)

BIG BRASS. This photograph taken in East Portland, Oregon, in 1883, shows a rare gathering of Northwest railroad officials and dignitaries. 1. W. H. Boot, Dist. Sup't., Pullman's Palace Car Co. 2. John H. Hallett, Sup't. of Construction, N. P. R. R. Co. 3. H. W. Fairweather, Sup't. , Pend d'Oreille Division, N. P. R. R. 4. John Muir, Sup't. of Traffic, O. R. & N. and N. P. R. R. Co. 5. Hans Thielsen, Chief Engineer, O. R. & N. Co. 6. Unidentified. 7. Henry Villard, President, O. R. & N. Co. and N. P. R. R. Co. 8. J. M. Buckley, Ass't. General Manager, N. P. R. R. Co. 9. U. S. Senator J. N. Dolph, Previously attorney for O. R. & N. Co. 10. Mr. Meade, member of firm McKim, Meade and White, New York architects. 11. C. A. Spofford, Private Secretary to Henry Villard. 12. P. Miescher, Hydraulic Engineer from Switzerland. 13. R. E. O'Brien, Engineer, Oregon & Transcontinental Co. Assistant Manager, O. R. & N. Co., Manager, N. P. T. Co. of Oregon. 14. Mr. Spiess, Hydraulic Engineer from Switzerland. 15. Richard Koehler, Vice President and Manager, O. & C. R. R. Co. 16. C. H. Prescott, Manager, O. R. & N. Co. 17. K. Van Oterendorp, Ex-Superintendent, Ocean Division, O. R. & N. Co. 18. James B. Fry, personal friend of Henry Villard and stockholder in Villard companies. On car platform, left to right: H. J. McDonald, Private Secretary to Mr. Thielsen. H. S. Rowe, Agent, O. R. & N. Portland Freight Station, later Superintendent. (Courtesy of Union Pacific Railroad)

NORTHERN PACIFIC FREIGHT CREW lined up for this photo near Juliaetta, Idaho, in the 1890's. The side-door caboose is typical of the waycars used in that era. The Baldwin 4-4-0, bearing road number 698, has been rebuilt with an extended front end and probably new dome casings. Note the unusual type of spokes in the leading wheel of the engine truck. The rimrock and barren hills are typical of the country traversed by the Northern Pacific line south of Kendrick. (Courtesy of Fred Jukes)

OREGON & CALIFORNIA RAILROAD Engine 1250, a three-domed Baldwin 4-4-0, is shown here at Portland in September, 1897, with a special consignment of merchandise to be turned over to the Oregon Railroad & Navigation Company for delivery to the Oregon Commercial Company at Huntington, Oregon. The Oregon & California Railroad extended from Portland south to Ashland, connecting there with the Southern Pacific's line to Dunsmuir, Sacramento, and the San Francisco Bay area. The funnel-stacked wood burner bore Baldwin Shop Number 2934, and was built in 1872 as the Oregon & California's No. 12. After the O. & C. was absorbed by the Southern Pacific, she was numbered S. P. 1505 and was scrapped in 1920. The engine had 16 x 24 inch cylinders and 63 inch drivers. (Courtesy of Henry R. Griffiths, Jr.)

TWO PASSENGER TRAINS operating on the Siskiyou Line of the Southern Pacific piled up in this head-on collision north of Black Butte, California, in the 1890's. Note the jumble of debris at the left, where the baggage and express cars have telescoped, scattering their contents. Engine 2843, at left, is a 4-8-0 cross-compound built by Schenectady in 1892; the 2800, leading engine of the doubleheader at right, was originally Central Pacific's 229, built at Sacramento in 1882, a 4-8-0 type. The road engine of the train at the far right is a diamond stack ten-wheeler, but her number is not visible.

7

Cornfield Meets And Assorted Catastrophes.

Train wrecks are not pleasant to look upon, but no story of early railroading along the Pacific Slope would be complete without some mention of them. Accurate data on accidents is very difficult to obtain, and for a number of reasons. Railroad management avoided mention of them for obvious reasons, and often the crews involved in them preferred to bury their ghastly memories. Old newspaper records are often inaccurate, even though they did give detailed coverage to many accidents that took place in the region.

Considering the nature of much of the terrain, the casual and often haphazard methods of operation, and lack of safety devices, the only wonder is that more accidents did not occur in the days when the West

A PAIR OF SOUTHERN PACIFIC LOCOMOTIVES are shown here after a head-on collision near Colton, California, in the link and pin days. Engine 105, the ten-wheeler squatting in the foreground, was built by Schenectady in 1880 as No. 25 of the Southern Pacific Railroad of Arizona. After several renumberings, she was sold to the Arizona Eastern in 1912. (G. M. Best collection, courtesy of David L. Joslyn)

NARROW GAUGE DERAILMENT occurred on the South Pacific Coast Railroad near Los Gatos, California. Engine 20 was a 4-6-0 built for the road by Baldwin in 1887 and ended her days on the 3-foot gauge lines of the Northwestern Pacific Railroad. Note the provision for three couplers on her pilot beam; center pocket contains a goose-neck link and left pocket is equipped with an automatic coupler. (Courtesy of Roy D. Graves)

FATAL MISHAP on the South Pacific Coast Railroad in the Santa Cruz Mountains near Wright's, California. Engine 17, a Baldwin 4-4-0, jumped the narrow gauge tracks and struck the side of a cut, killing Engineer Jim Stanley. The derby hat of the unfortunate runner can be noted on the deck beneath the reverse lever quadrant in the shattered cab. (Courtesy of Ron Hughes, Hughes Photo Service)

SACRAMENTO & PLACERVILLE RAILROAD pile-up near Folsom, California, was evidently caused by a derailment. Only scant information is available, but the pilot of the overturned 4-4-0 is intact, ruling out the possibility of a head-on collision. The tank is upside down and the wooden cab badly crushed, but perhaps the crew had time to unload before the old gal landed in the ditch. (Collection of the late J. W. S. Butler, courtesy of D. L. Joslyn)

NATURE LOVER, this Southern Pacific 4-6-0 left the rails in search of greener pastures and, after sauntering through a hedge, came to rest on the velvet lawn of a park. Steam sizzles from the old gal's pop valves as a crowd of curious spectators mill around the palms and yuccas. The locale and costumes indicate the mishap took place in California in the 1890's. (John Paulson collection, courtesy P. M. Theobald and H. H. Arey)

and its railroads were young.

Some of the operating mishaps, where no injuries were involved, often had a humorous twist. Take the case of the sleepy engineer assigned to helper service on one Western pike. After having boosted a train up to a mountain summit, this runner and another helper crew turned their locomotives and dropped back down the hill to their home terminal. Business was brisk on the road, and they were informed that they would be used to help a second train as soon as their engines could be turned. The two helpers, coupled together, were headed into a track leading onto the turntable and while awaiting an opportunity to turn the power, the engineer on the rear locomotive cocked his feet up on the Johnson bar and dozed off. A short time later, the engineer on a train occupying the main line nearby whistled off. The drowsing helper engineer, roused from his nap and forgetting for the moment where he was, rapped out two short answering blasts on his whistle, widened on his throttle and shoved the helper engine coupled ahead of him into the turntable pit!

Some accidents were caused by human carelessness, but the great majority of them were caused by circumstances beyond the control of the crews involved. Livestock roamed at large on the vast open ranges and created a constant menace until right-of-ways were fenced. A stray cow upset a woodburner on the West Side line of the Oregon & California Railroad, and a big range bull, disputing the passage of a narrow gauge train on the Nevada-California-Oregon, caused a wreck that killed the engineer. A Southern Pacific passenger train, drawn by a small ten-wheeler, struck a bull lying on the tracks near Junction City, Oregon, not long after the turn of the century. Fireman Frank H. Bolter was crushed under the locomotive, and Engineer Jack Nichols was so severely scalded that he died in the arms of his rescuers.

Many old-time runners dreaded hitting the bands of sheep that often grazed onto the tracks. The woolly carcasses had a tendency to pile up under the pony trucks, resulting in derailment of the light motive power. Joseph Clark, a veteran Oregon & California Railroad engineer, struck a band of sheep in 1889, killing 90 of them. In the pile-up that followed, he was so seriously cut about the face and eyes by broken glass from the shattered cab windows that he lost his eyesight, a tragedy that later broke his mind.

A bull ended the railroad career of Oregon Railway & Navigation Company runner Charlie Evans. Coming into East Portland on Train No. 1, his passenger locomotive struck a bull and a side rod broke. The flailing end the fractured rod

155

cleaned the right side of the cab, breaking Engineer Evans' leg and so crippling him that he was forced to give up his job.

A Northern Pacific express train, rushing silk and tea to the East Coast, struck a cow at Toppenish, Washington, shortly after the Cascade line was completed. The impact hurled old Bossy through the bay window of the frame depot and the engine crew often wondered what the agent's reactions were when he opened the door the following morning and found a hamburgered bovine strewn over his depot floor.

Nature often stacked the cards against the puny efforts of railroaders, sending slides, floods, and sand drifts to create hazards for the operating personnel to combat. Many roads in the Northwest and in the timbered regions of California passed through dense forests, and the construction crews cut a swath in the timber just wide enough to accommodate the right-of-way. From the stands of trees left adjacent, winds often toppled huge giants of the forest across the rails. A South Pacific Coast Railroad engine struck a big redwood that had fallen across the tracks and broken in two, high in the Santa Cruz Mountains. The engine crew tried to stop before striking the obstruction, but the locomotive hit the tree and was so securely wedged between the broken sections of the fallen log that it had to be chopped free.

The old style oil headlights, used for many years, failed to provide sufficient illumination and contributed to many accidents. One veteran runner, questioned about the merits of these lamps, gave the writer this reply. "Oil headlights? Hell, yes, I should say I do remember them. They throwed a yellow glow about thirty feet ahead of you, and gave just enough light to see to get killed by!"

This statement was all too true. The dim glow, resembling a full moon when seen from ahead, often illuminated a rock, slide, or fallen tree too late to permit the crew to bring their train to a halt.

On a Sunday evening, August 15th, 1897, a freight train was rambling down Cow Creek Canyon, on the old line of the Oregon & California Railroad. Engineer Ernie Stroud and Fireman Robert McEwan were in the cab of the 1758, a 2-6-0 woodburner, and the head brakeman, J. N. Flook, was sitting up on the tool box on the tank. Conductor Al Morris and the other two brakemen, Ben Maddox and Ralph Knight, were riding in the caboose. The freight was dangling along at a lively pace, as the northbound Overland Limited was running about 2 hours late and the freight crew was attempting to run into Roseburg ahead of them. It was a beautiful autumn night, typical of southern Oregon, with a haze of wood smoke in the balmy air and a brilliant full moon lighting up the wild reaches of the canyon. About 11:30 P. M., nearing Union Creek,

A STRAY COW grazing on the right-of-way of the San Francisco & North Pacific Railway put Engine 23 and a passenger train in the ditch on October 29th, 1911. Fireman George Gilliam was badly scalded in this derailment, which took place between Cloverdale and Ukiah, California. (L. S. Slevin collection, courtesy of Roy D. Graves)

PACIFIC RAILWAY & NAVIGATION CO. line near Timber, Oregon, was the scene of this 1910 derailment. The locomotive is No. 1355 of the Southern Pacific, but was originally No. 22 of the Oregon & California Railroad. Conductor J. G. Griffiths stands in the foreground, foot on rail, with Brakeman Gay Worthington at his left. Fireman Chet Alexander is standing on the tank truck and Engineer Al Wagner is leaning against the engine beneath the cab. The car in front of the locomotive is a wood rack, for transporting the mountains of slab and cord wood used by Northwest householders for cooking and heating before gas and electricity came into common use. (Courtesy of Ben W. Griffiths)

Engineer Stroud glimpsed a cloud of dust swirling down a steep bank ahead. His first thought was that cattle were running across the track toward the creek; as the engine drew closer, he saw the dust was caused by a huge fir stump that had burned off and was rolling down onto the track. The oil headlight had been too weak to pick out the obstruction, and only the bright moonlight revealed the stump lying on the rails. Despite a desperate attempt to stop, the engine hit the stump and plunged over the embankment into the shallow waters of Cow Creek, followed by four or five cars. Engineer Stroud was thrown into the stream and Brakeman Flook was tossed clear, both men being fortunate to escape with minor bruises. Fireman McEwan was not so lucky; pinned in the shattered wooden cab, he suffered a broken arm and steam from a ruptured injector pipe scalded him badly. When Stroud climbed into the debris searching for him, McEwan greeted him with these words, "I've always liked the 1758 and now she has killed me." His prophetic words were true. Conductor Morris had hurried back to West Fork station afoot, returning with a light engine he found there, also bringing down the West Fork section gang. A wrecker special was hurried to the scene from Roseburg, bearing Trainmaster George Estes and Doctor J. C. Twitchell.

McEwan was freed from the wrecked cab, but the scalding steam had done its deadly work, searing the poor lad's lungs. He died on the depot platform as the special delivered him in Roseburg, some 15 hours after the wreck occurred. He left a young wife and an infant son to mourn his passing. The son grew up in his father's footsteps and is now an engineer on the Portland Division of the Southern Pacific.

Supt. L. R. Fields and Master Mechanic T. W. Younger hurried from Portland to the site of the wreck to supervise clearing the road. A temporary spur had to be built down to the 1758 and it was not until the following Wednesday that the engine was pulled out of the stream and towed to the shops for repairs. Built by Baldwin in 1883 as the Ore. & Cal. R. R. No. 39, she later became S. P. 1611.

A fallen tree once imperiled a Northern Pacific passenger train speeding through the timbered region of western Washington but as Fate would have it, only minor damage resulted. The crack flyer left Ellensburg about 9:00 P. M. one night, running 25 minutes late. The train, consisting of 10 coaches, was in charge of Conductor Paul Thompson. Engineer Harvey Reed and Fireman Sam Hood manned the high-wheeled passenger engine. Reed pounded the old gal on the back as they

REAR END COLLISION occurred in the yards at Grants Pass, Oregon, in 1906. Train No. 16, hauled by two diamond stack 4-6-0's, rammed into the rear of a freight projecting out onto the main line in a dense fog. Fireman John Barger was crushed to death when the engine on the point jack-knifed against her tender. The passenger locomotives plowed through a box car loaded with cased dynamite, which fortunately did not explode. Siskiyou line traffic was routed around the debris on a shoo-fly built behind Engine 2192, the passenger road engine at the far right.

climbed out of the Kittitas Valley and topped the Cascade Range, then soared down the western slope. The varnish roared along the shores of the Green River, dashing across the flats and arriving at South Prairie only 10 minutes off schedule. The runner hooked the Johnson bar up and was hitting 70 miles per hour in an effort to make up the lost time before arriving in Tacoma, the end of the run. In a dense stand of timber, the headlight suddenly picked up the outline of a broken tree projecting across the track about level with the smokebox. Reed big-holed the air and hossed her over, but they hit and hit hard. The two-foot thick log stove in the front end and the left main rod of the engine was kinked, but the train was able to proceed slowly. Superintendent McCabe was watching as the crippled engine struggled up the grade into the Avenue Depot in Tacoma. He saw the fire flying from the ruptured smokebox and later told Engineer Reed that the spectacle looked like a little hell with the lid off.

In the days of wooden passenger equipment and wood or coal stoves for car heating purposes, train wrecks often ended in grisly conflagrations. The old style coal oil lamps used for illuminating the cars contributed to these fiery holocausts. In January, 1883 a Central Pacific passenger train stopped on the steep Tehachapi grade and the locomotive was cut off to take water. Before a sufficient number of

hand brakes could be tied down, the train began to inch away back down the steep grade. Despite the frantic efforts of the train crew, the speed began to increase and soon reached a terrifying rate. The runaway finally left the track and piled up, killing four passengers outright and injuring 14 others. Most of those injured suffered burns of varying degrees from the fire that broke out before rescuers could free them from the tangled debris.

While loss of life by fire in the train wrecks of early days was an expected hazard, death by drowning was infrequent but not unknown. A South Pacific Coast passenger train, with Engineer S. Dunn at the latch, plunged into the Oakland, California, Estuary when the Webster Street drawbridge was opened to allow a boat to pass, drowning a large number of unfortunate passengers. A similar accident befell the interurban East Side Railway when the car *Inez* skidded through an open draw span into the Willamette River in Portland in 1893, drowning seven.

While the wrecks involving road crews were more spectacular, it is probable that more injuries to employees were incurred in yard switching. The details of these accidents are buried in the files of many companies, but in the early days of railroading countless numbers of switchmen were killed or maimed. The link and pin coupler was a notorious collector of fingers and hands, and the unblocked

ASTORIA & COLUMBIA RIVER'S No. 7, a Rogers 4-4-0 of 1883 vintage, flipped over on her left side near Columbia City, Oregon, on December 2nd, 1910. Originally Oregon Pacific Railroad's No. 2, she was taken to the Columbia River road by A. B. Hammond in 1896 and later became No. 54 of the Spokane, Portland & Seattle Railway. (Courtesy of John T. Labbe)

frogs waited to trap the feet of the careless or the hurried. The oil lanterns furnished only feeble light, and many a switchman was "rolled," caught in insufficient clearance between cars and crushed to death.

On many of the early pikes, in the days before rigid safety rules and Government inspection, broken grab-irons and stirrups were common; yardmen, grabbing a fast-moving car in the dark, often fell victim to these hazards. The man who caught a weakened handhold was lucky if he fell clear, rather than under the murderous wheels. Rail terminals throughout the West were filled with the victims of railroad switching accidents. Men who lost limbs in the service were sometimes retained as crossing watchmen, while others were often set up in small businesses through the assistance of their fellow rails. Brakeman Johnny Young, riding a flat car being shoved ahead of a work train engine on the old Oregon Pacific, leaped to the hand brake when cattle appeared around a curve. The brake chain broke, as they had a habit of doing, and Young fell across the rail in front of the car, losing both legs. When he had recovered from his injuries, the Oregon Pacific rewarded him for his loss by giving him the news agent's franchise on their passenger trains and he was long a familiar sight to travellers as he peddled his merchandise aboard the cars.

Boiler explosions claimed the lives of a number of engine crews in bygone years. In the Southwest, bad water was a constant problem, and low water alarms, fusible "drop" or "soft" plugs, and frequent boiler inspections were in the distant future. Engine No. 17, named the *Idaho,* had her boiler extended in the Central Pacific shops at Ogden and on her second trip out, early in 1879, she blew up, killing both engineer and fireman. An earlier explosion destroyed a Central Pacific locomotive at Clipper Gap in 1868. The first locomotive of the Los Angeles & San Pedro scattered her tiny boiler over the landscape at San Pedro in 1869 and the solitary motive power on the Petaluma & Haystack Railroad had exploded her boiler at the Petaluma station earlier, killing her engineer and three others on August 27th, 1866.

The *L. L. Robinson* of the Sacramento Valley Railroad blew up at Folsom, Californa, ending the career of one of the earliest locomotives on the Pacific Coast.

Being blown to glory from the wooden cabs of their iron horses was not a fate restricted to enginemen in the southern regions. Bellingham Bay & British Columbia's Engine No. 6 dropped her crown sheet on Cougar Hill in 1905 and Engine No. 4 of the same road lost her crown sheet at Sumas, Washington, killing her fireman. The latter explosion occurred after the road had been reorganized as the Bellingham & Northern.

Southern Pacific's Consolidation type No. 2538 blew up while ascending Rice Hill in helper service, the year being 1912. Enginer Bartlett and Fireman Adderton both died when the hog scattered her boiler over the Oregon hillside, and another Southern Pacific engineman met death when his locomotive blew up on the steep Siskiyou grade near Ashland, Oregon. The same road lost Engine 2116, a ten-wheeler, in an explosion on the Lucin Cutoff in 1904, while their Consolidation No. 2617 blew up at Gold Run, California, in 1906. Bigger engines suffered the same fate: No. 4037, a cab-forward 2-8-8-2 blew up in 1914 and another cab-forward, No. 4199, went skyward near Salinas in 1941.

The crew of an Oregon Railway & Navigation Co. eight-wheeler had the distinction of surviving a boiler explosion. Engineer John Burns and Fireman English were manning Engine 67 one fine morning in 1910 on the run between Wallula and Walla Walla, Washington. Without warning, the wrapper sheet of the boiler let go and the pieces, including bell, sand dome and stack, went sailing out over the sage brush, some fragments landing half a mile away. The engine and the train's two passenger cars were derailed, but remained upright, and neither crew nor passengers were injured.

In the days prior to the general application of the air brake to cars and engines, the mountain roads of the West were the scenes of many runaways. A freight train crew, arriving at the Summit station of the Southern Pacific's Sierra Nevada route in the early 1890's, cut off the engine and before enough hand brakes could be set to hold it, the train

began to roll back down the steep grade. The trainmen fought desperately to bring the cars to a halt but their efforts were in vain. Gaining in momentum at every turn of the wheels, the runaway freight roared down the western slope of the Sierra. Some five miles downgrade from Summit was the little telegraph and train order office called Cascade. The station building contained living quarters for the telegraph operator, and was perched on the edge of the tracks above a steep canyon, the rear of the structure being supported by stilt-like timbering. The speed of the runaway had increased terrifically and the flying cars left the rails just as they neared the Cascade office. The telegrapher, one J. B. Dorsey, was in bed when the derailed freight struck the station and demolished it. The telegrapher was tossed some forty feet down the bank of the canyon but was not seriously injured. The train crew, still valiantly sticking to their posts at the brake staffs, were hurtled to death in the awful jumble of wreckage in the gorge below. The musty stacks of early newspapers are filled with similar disasters.

Before the automatic air brake came into use it was a common occurrence for a train to break in two. Sometimes the break would be unnoticed by the engine crew and the head end of the train would stop, only to be rammed by the detached rear portion. If ascending a grade, the cars that broke free would roll back down the mountain until they derailed or struck a following train.

One of the longest runaways in Western history had a happy ending. A Northern Pacific freight

RESERVATION WRECK shows a ten-wheeler of the Oregon Railroad & Navigation Company with her boiler head submerged after plunging into the Umatilla River east of Pendleton, Oregon, on April 10th, 1907. The wreck site is near Cayuse station, on the Umatilla Indian Reservation, and a group of Indians are surveying the debris from a vantage point on the cut bank in the right background. This photo was taken by Major Lee Moorhouse, noted for his fine pictures of Indians and action shots of the famed Pendleton Roundup. (Courtesy of Oregon Collection, University of Oregon)

DEATH RODE THE RAILS when this 4-6-0 dropped through a flood-weakened bridge over Willow Creek on the Union Pacific's Heppner Branch in Eastern Oregon. Engineer Sam Hansen, a boomer of wide experience, was killed here and his body was pinned beneath his engine for several days. Also killed was Section Foreman Habelt, while the fireman was thrown into the stream but escaped serious injury. Engine 1716 was built by Cooke in 1890 as O. R. & N. No. 137. (Courtesy of Ben W. Griffiths)

COLUMBIA & PUGET SOUND RAILROAD'S Engine No. 4, a diamond stack 2-6-0, had the misfortune to leave the narrow gauge rails and topple over near May Creek, Washington. Details regarding this wreck have evidently been lost with the passage of time, but such mishaps were commonplace in the bygone days when the West and its railroads were both young. (Courtesy of C. W. Mendenhall)

pulled into Yakima, Washington, in the 1890's and cut off the engine to pick up some cars loaded with cattle. The brakemen were all engaged in this chore, since it was necessary to make a drop or flying switch in order to get the loaded cars out of the stock track and onto the train. The conductor remained in the caboose, intending to tie down enough brakes to hold the train until the engine could be re-coupled. However, that worthy promptly fell asleep and when the brakemen returned with the loads to couple up, they found their train missing. Cautiously backing through the night, they eased down the main line. Their train had been displaying signals for a following section and the crew expected to find a frightful jumble of wreckage around every curve. Thirty miles east of Yakima, the gentle down grade ended and the rails began to ascend and it was in this sag that they found their missing train. Only the fact that the second section was running some two hours late had averted a bad pile-up.

The oldtime crews did everything in their power to prevent wrecks, often sticking to the post of duty

NORTHERN PACIFIC TRAIN No. 1, hauled by Engine 440, piled up between Missoula and Bonner, Montana, in 1889. Engineer S. H. Draper escaped injury and later became the road's first Air Brake Superintendent. Draper had been at the throttle of one of the special trains operated to the Northern Pacific's last spike ceremonies at Gold Creek; the Mullan Tunnel had not been completed at that time and the trains crossed the summit of the Continental Divide on a series of steep switchbacks. (Courtesy of Ronald V. Nixon)

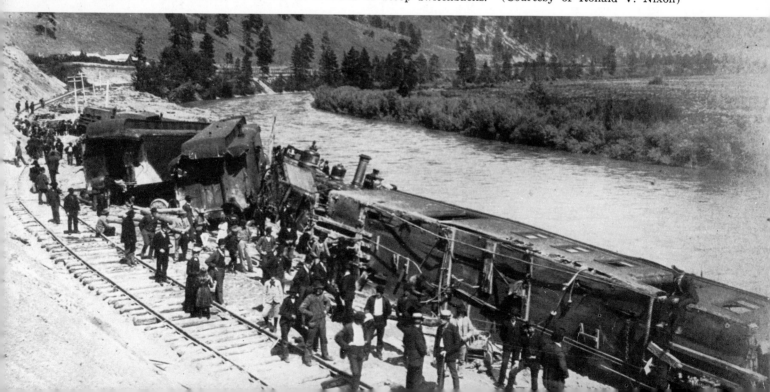

NORTHERN PACIFIC'S ENGINE 764 rolled down the bank near Florence, Montana, in 1899, killing Engineer Beebe. The 4-4-0 was running on the branch extending south from Missoula to Grantsdale. Ten wheeler No. 356 is shown with hand-operated wrecking crane No. 9 in the background. (Courtesy of Ronald V. Nixon)

until it was too late to save their own lives. This devotion to duty was not limited to train and engine crews, by any means. When a flash flood swept the village of Heppner, Oregon, in June, 1903, Agent Kernan started his family to a place of safety on the surrounding hills then hurried back to his telegraph key in the doomed station. His message of warning to the other villages located downstream along the O. R. & N. branch line was never sent. A wall of water crushed the wooden depot and claimed the life of this brave railroader.

With the passing years, the railroads of the West became more safety conscious, and wrecks happily became fewer and less disastrous. Better bridges, heavier rail, regular inspection of equipment, block signals, and, perhaps the most important of all, air brakes were the factors that helped end the costly smashes that often had such tragic endings. The rail lines of the Pacific Slope are today among the safest in the nation, with a wonderful record of accident-free operation.

SEATTLE & INTERNATIONAL RAILROAD log train fell 110 feet into Raging River when this wooden trestle collapsed on May 15th, 1900. Engineer William Farr was killed and Fireman John Marion, now a retired Northern Pacific engineer, was seriously injured. The road is now the North Bend Branch of the Northern Pacific. (John Marion collection, courtesy of Benj. T. Hart)

NORTHERN PACIFIC'S ENGINE 649 was rounding a sharp curve at Monohan, Washington, with a log train when the unprotected rear end of the local freight loomed up. Engineer William A. Dahlberg dove out the right gangway, scrambled up the bank and escaped through the wire fence in the foreground just as a load of logs shot by his heels. Fireman Anton Rylea joined the birds from the opposite gangway, and no one was injured. The crew of the local was switching the Monohan mill when this accident took place around 1906-07. (A. T. Knowles collection, courtesy of Benj. T. Hart)

NORTHERN PACIFIC trains met head-on at Woodinville, Washington, in 1912, killing a baggage man and badly injuring a mail clerk. Engine No. 90, a Rome 2-8-0, was pulling out of the siding with the North Bend local freight when she was struck head-on by Engine No. 351, at right, a Baldwin ten-wheeler pulling the varnish from Sumas to Seattle. (Courtesy of Benj. T. Hart)

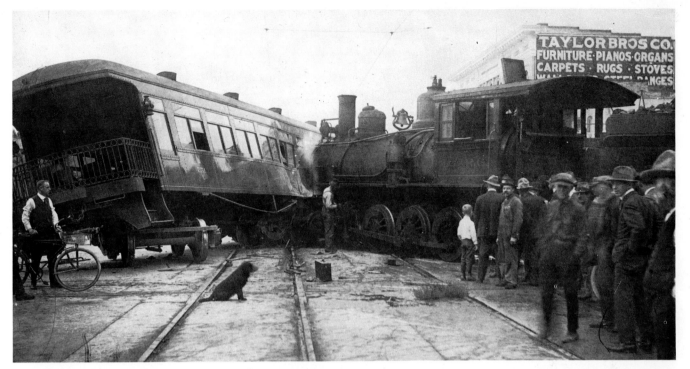

OBSERVATION CAR of the interurban Salt Lake & Utah Railroad was rammed in the side by a Denver & Rio Grande hog on Center Street in Provo, Utah, around 1918. This view of the crash, looking west, is from an original glass plate negative. The Rio Grande engine, pulling a Heber train, has parted from her tender and shows her extended boiler head that came back flush with the rear wall of the cab. Provo's Salt Lake & Utah Valley Railroad was the successor to the West Side Rapid Transit Company, operating electric and steam dummy lines. (Courtesy of F. D. Fellow)

REAR END COLLISION at Boise, Idaho, on October 20th, 1908, claimed the life of one man aboard Oregon Short Line's No. 405. The eight-wheeler was leaving Boise, bound for Nampa, when she collided with the rear of a special fair train being backed down to the Boise depot. The tender of the 405 has jammed up against the boiler head and the nose of the engine is buried in the coach at right. (Courtesy of Henry Griffiths, Jr.)

FALLEN MONARCHS OF THE FOREST, these huge sections of redwood logs are ready to roll to the mill behind the woodburning 0-4-4 saddletanker. The locomotive is equipped with a "spool" engine mounted on the pilot beam, the drum of which is visible above the right cylinder. Shed at the right, beyond the loaded bunks, houses the steam donkey used for moving the giant logs to the landing for loading. The ravaged hillside in the background clearly shows the stark desolation left in the wake of the redwood loggers. (Courtesy of Jack Slattery, Jack's Photo Service)

Logs and Lokeys.

More precious than the golden nuggets in the economy of the region west of the Rockies was and is the green gold that spread like a blanket over valley floor and mountain range. The first settlers in the Northwest found the timber a detriment, and only a very little of it was processed for local use or for export. The Hudson's Bay Company established a crude sawmill at Fort Vancouver and shipped some of the rough planks to the Sandwich Islands in what was probably the first lumbering venture for commercial gain on the Pacific Coast.

Vast areas of the region were densely forested with firs, interspersed with stands of hemlock, cedar and spruce. East of the Cascades, and throughout the Sierras, magnificent sweeps of pine marched in

FORT BRAGG RAILROAD'S No. 1 was a 2-4-2 Baldwin saddle tank built in the mid-1880's. This California lumber road hauler had 42 inch drivers, 12 x 20 inch cylinders, and a working boiler pressure of 130 pounds. She later became Fort Bragg Lumber Company No. 1, then California Western Railroad's No. 1, but is shown here as she appeared under her original ownership, bearing the name SEQUOIA. The contraption mounted on her frame in front of the smokebox is a steam-powered "spool" engine, an auxiliary device handy for yarding logs off the track, rerailing cars, etc. (Union Lumber Company collection, courtesy of Ralph W. Andrews)

park-line panoramas, and in California the giant sequoia awed the pioneer with its unbelievable size.

Beautiful to look upon, the rain forests choked the hills and valleys and the early settlers cursed the growth as they strove mightily to clear the land for cultivation. Thousands of feet of fine timber went up in the smoke of land-clearing fires while the demand for lumber steadily increased. Soon the bellow of bull teams echoed down the sun-dappled forest aisles as the early loggers skid-roaded logs to primitive mills, and the crash of falling timber startled the denizens of the wilderness.

As the hungry saws whined and the pungent sawdust piled up, the slow plodding of the ox teams began to hamper the industry. It was not long before steam began to replace water power in the sawmills and loggers began casting a speculative eye on this new power that did not eat expensive hay and grain, but could consume the waste wood and convert it into energy.

The history of logging railroading is obscured in the mists of West Coast yesteryears. Unauthenticated reports hint at the existence of a steam locomotive hauling logs around the Coos Bay tidelands as early as 1853. However, it was not until several decades later that logging by rail really came into widespread practice. Up on Puget Sound, the dinky

engines of the Satsop Railroad were trundling logs to the Shelton dumping grounds in 1884 and Simon Benson, Columbia River logger, began thrusting rails into his timber near Cathlamet in the 1890's.

However, most of the pioneer logging railroad operations centered in California's redwood region. Logs moved into Arcata over tramways pulled by horses, and steam locomotives soon replaced the equine motive power. In the 1870's, railroads were tapping the timber around Eureka, Samoa, and Humboldt Bay. The Arcata & Mad River Railroad, the Humboldt Bay & Trinidad, and the Fort Bragg Railroad all moved timber in the 1880's.

The various companies that operated logging railways were so numerous as to almost defy identification; when timber was cut out, the entire equipment of a line was frequently moved to a fresh stand of timber and operations resumed under another name. Some of the roads were more permanent and reached the status of common carriers, while others operated as a strictly private pike for the convenience of their owners. Not a few of the pioneer roads were incorporated into larger systems and the Eel River & Eureka, opened out of Field's Landing in 1884, formed a part of the present Northwestern Pacific, along with other logging lines.

The assortment of motive power that was pressed

into logging road operations is wondrous to contemplate. Discarded rod engines acquired second-hand from regular railroads stormed along the sketchy tracks between many camps and mills, hauling logs and lumber long after having outlived their usefulness on main line runs. Shiny new locomotives, fresh from the builders' paint shops, sent their exhaust skyward to obscure the towering fir and pine. Steam "dummy" types, driven from street and suburban railways by electricity, found homes in the big woods; even a number of Forney types that had served the elevated lines of Eastern metropolises were shipped out to haul logs in their declining years. When the Mount Hood Railroad was being built to serve the mills of the Oregon Lumber Company out of Hood River, Oregon, in the winter of 1905-6, Art Sayre recalls that the construction engine he fired was a small 2-4-2 steam dummy that was formerly used on street railways in Ogden, Utah. This kettle had no water glass, and the fireman had to try the gauge cocks frequently to avoid blowing her to Kingdom Come. Like many of her sister engines in logging road service, she burned slab wood, a by-product of sawmilling that offered cheap fuel.

The real glamor girls of the logging pikes, however, were the geared locomotives that were designed to operate on steep grades and poor track. These geared engines were of three types: the Shay, the Climax, and the Heisler. The Shay was a lop-sided creature developed in the pines around the Great Lakes, but its characteristics proved it desirable for use in the Pacific forests. The engine was driven by cylinders mounted vertically on the right side of the boiler, power being transmitted to the wheels by a line shaft and gears. To compensate for the weight of the cylinders and driving gear, the boiler was mounted off center on the left of the frame, giving the locomotive an odd appearance when viewed head-on. These engines could climb grades that would stop an ordinary rod locomotive cold, and their flexibility made them easy on the track.

The Heisler and the Climax were also gear-driven and offered the same advantages. The former had a pair of cylinders mounted V-fashion under the belly of the boiler to connect with the shaft; the Climax sported a set of cylinders mounted at the saddle in the manner of conventional locomotives, only at a different angle. Rods from the crossheads were connected to a flywheel affair, which in turn transmitted power to a center line shaft and gears. Use of these three types of geared locomotives made it possible to lay rail into remote regions where ordinary locomotives could not operate, and the loggers lost no time in claiming these iron mules for their work. Grades on lines using geared engines were almost unbelievably steep, and curves so short that long logs often rubbed the side of the cut when passing around them.

No resume of logging railroading would be complete without mention of the locomotives built by

NARROW GAUGE LOGGING ENGINE, this little Porter 0-6-0 operated on James Doherty's Extension Railroad, running from a connection with the South Pacific Coast Railroad at Boulder Creek, California, up to Doherty's Mill and on into the big timber of the Santa Cruz Mountains. The locomotive is believed to have come from the Santa Cruz & Felton Railroad, a short line operated between Santa Cruz and Old Felton in 1875. (Courtesy of Ronnie Hughes, Hughes Photo Service)

STEAM WAS KING in the woods that bewhiskered the Pacific Empire. From the California redwoods to the pines of Arizona and Idaho and up through the evergreen rain forests of Oregon and Washington, logs poured into the saw mills over the shining rails. The 4-Spot of California's McCloud River Railroad is depicted here with a heavy drag of pine logs, her tank piled high with wood for her hungry firebox. (Lew Parsons collection, courtesy of Collier State Park Logging Museum)

the Willamette Iron & Steel Company of Portland, Oregon. This firm built donkey engines that were widely used in logging operations and in 1922 they turned out a Shay-type locomotive for use on a logging railroad. This first geared engine was built for the Coos Bay Lumber Co. and bore the road number 10. Like many new products, she had some mechanical kinks that had to be ironed out but she was a success and the Willamette Iron & Steel lokeys became a common sight in the logging camps along the Pacific Slope. A few of them survive to this day, although steam in the woods is becoming as rare as the cigar store Indian of yesteryear.

The common type of disconnected "bunk" used on many logging lines made the use of air brakes impossible, and the long heavy trains were eased down mountainsides by brakemen skilled in the use of hand brakes. Even with the exercise of utmost caution runaways frequently sent log trains roaring to destruction, sometimes with results that were humorous rather than fatal.

Engineer Miller's crew lost control of their Shay-drawn cargo of logs descending a steep grade in

WEED LUMBER COMPANY'S No. 3, husky 2-8-0 wood burner with a diamond stack, trails a train of pine out of the forests of Northern California around 1900. The 3-Spot's boiler extended back flush with the rear wall of the cab, entrance to the interior being gained through doors on each side of the boiler. The short pine logs were chained to the cars to enable larger loads to be carried out to the mills. (Bill Tingley collection, courtesy of Collier State Park Logging Museum)

the lower Columbia River region. The crew judiciously bailed off when it became apparent that the situation was beyond human effort, but in the excitement they neglected to toss off the engineer's pet dog, a constant companion of Miller's who loved to ride in the cab. The crash of breaking equipment soon told them that their train had failed to negotiate a sharp curve and the crew walked down the grade to view the wreckage. The Shay was a pile of smoking scrap, buried under a jumble of huge logs at the bottom of a steep canyon. The men whistled and called, hoping the dog might have survived the final plunge, but got no response. They guessed that poor old Shep had made his last run and was beyond human help in the twisted, steam-filled mass in the canyon, so they sadly trudged back to camp to report the runaway. Upon arriving, they found old Shep seated at the cook-house door, covered with oil but uninjured. The dog had remained in the cab until the engine had overturned, spilling fuel oil from the tank over him, but had escaped and taken a short cut back through the timber, beating the crew to camp.

Most early logging camps were of a temporary nature built to last until the timber was cut off,

MECHANICAL MONSTER, this little engine of odd design was built in 1909 at a foundry in Eureka, California, for the Bayside Lumber Company. An 0-4-4-0 type, her cylinders were cast separately and bolted to the frame; this led to a great deal of trouble, as the cylinders would work loose and cut the packing, as well as distorting the valve motion. The end came for this nameless, numberless little pot in 1911 when her crew was descending a 3% grade with a train of logs and no air. Losing control, they prudently unloaded in a sand bank and let the runaway go to its doom without human casualty. The engine left the rails on a 16 degree curve on a trestle, fell 65 feet, and was so badly broken up that she was scrapped.

then the entire outfit would move on to the next location. A cluster of rough board shacks, a cook-house, blacksmith shop, and perhaps a barn-like shed for housing the locomotives, these constituted a typical logging camp. Some outfits had their living quarters built on railroad cars after the fash-

PINE COUNTRY PIONEER, this little Baldwin 0-4-2 was No. 1 of the Pokegama Sugar Pine Lumber Company and was called OLD BLUE. The engine was freighted in to the logging road by oxen or horses from Klamathon, California, in 1891. Five to seven loaded cars of logs were dropped down from the woods by gravity to the head of a log chute leading into the Klamath River; after the logs were dumped, OLD BLUE hauled the empty cars back into the timber. The teen-aged engineer in the cab is Bud Inman, while Brakeman Frank Woods stands at the brake staff on the cars; the gent by the cylinder is Ed Way, woods boss and general factotum of the logging operation. (Hal Ogle collection, courtesy of Collier State Park Logging Museum)

THROUGH THE PASTORAL MEADOWS of Oregon's Coos County rolls old No. 1, the NORTH BEND, trailing three loads of fir logs across a low trestle; Engineer Bickford is handling her throttle as her pop valve blows and fog obscures the timbered coastal hills. The logging firm of McDonald & Vaughan operated this road to haul logs for A. M. Simpson's sawmill. The 1-Spot, of unknown origin, has an unusual metal cover placed over her headlight to protect the glass. This engine was involved in a tragedy when the wife of the engineer, attempting to board the train, was thrown under a car and killed.

172

ion of early railroad construction gangs; when a move was necessary, a lokey was coupled into the string of bunk and work cars and away went the whole shebang to a new camp spur.

At a Conlough Company camp in the Coos Bay area, the one-armed engineer lost control of his Shay and the runaway came roaring into camp just before the cook's "gut-hammer" was to signal the call to eat. The cook-house in this camp hugged the main stem and the Shay picked the spot to jump the track. The building and the hearty meal spread on the plank tables was reduced to kindling and garbage.

In the Yaquina region, another logging camp used by the Spruce Division during the first World War had a huge Army-style latrine bordering the main line. Engineer 'Dolph Peterson was letting his Shay clatter through camp at a lively gait with a string of empty bunks when suddenly his "side-winder" bounced violently over a broken rail. The Shay made it across the break, but the empty bunks hit the ties and headed for the latrine. The structure was demolished, a number of sets of trucks buried in the pit, and the unsavory mess earned Engineer Peterson an unprintable monicker that stuck with him as long as he handled a latch on logging locomotives.

The late Albert H. Powers, affectionately called "Uncle Al" by his crews of timber beasts, moved into the tall firs of Oregon's Coos County after years of cutting pines around the Great Lakes. His logging railroads reached into an evergreen empire of virgin timber and soon long drags of giant trees were rolling to the mills over Powers' steel. "Uncle Al" had a phenomenal memory and was noted for his colorful speech. One day he visited a crew engaged in fencing a section of his right-of-way and broke off his conversation with the foreman to stare at a workman engaged in erecting the fence. He recognized the man as a former cook he had fired for stealing supplies. Turning to the foreman, he queried, "Isn't that crooked so and so up there John Doe? The foreman replied in the affirmative and asked Powers if the man was really crooked. "Is he crooked?" Powers choked, "Oh, watch him, watch him like a hawk. He'd steal Christ off the Cross and then come back for the nails!"

PICTURESQUE LOGGING SHOW at the Bridal Veil Lumber Company operations in Oregon combined logging railroading and fluming. An 0-6-0 Baldwin saddle tanker is crossing the trestle over the flume in the background, a string of logs being snaked along the track behind her pilot beam. Note that the trestle is solidly decked with ties to permit logs to be skidded between the rails without using cars, a method of operation reputedly inaugurated by this outfit. The "high lead" style of logging with cable and donkey engine is also reported to have originated on this former ox-team logging show.

ELK CREEK RAILROAD rolls a long drag of redwoods down to the mill at Elk, Mendocino County, California, across a typical logging road trestle. The little 0-4-0 saddle tank coupled next to the logs is being doubleheaded by a Baldwin 4-4-0 of 1874 vintage; formerly No. 1, the SAUCELITO, of the narrow gauge North Pacific Coast, she was owned by the L. E. White Lumber Company, located at Elk. (Courtesy of Roy D. Graves)

Logging railroaders in general were a colorful lot, tough, resourceful and rugged. Many of them were "outlaws", fired off main line roads for such exuberances as drinking on duty or poking official noses.

Alfred D. Collier, Klamath Basin lumberman who has preserved locomotives and logging equipment for posterity in the Collier State Park Logging Museum near Chiloquin, Oregon, recounts an episode involving Rule G on a Klamath logging railroad. The engineer on this pike was returning to camp with a string of empty cars and a bottle of wood alcohol for his wife's chafing dish. Pounding along upgrade, he felt the need of a charge of liquid refreshment and fumbled around in the tank box for a bottle of Old Crow he carried there. In the dim light of the cab lamp, he hauled out the bottle and downed a mighty slug, discovering too late that he had laid hands on the bottle of lethal wood alcohol. The quick-witted fireboy came to his rescue, pouring down the engineer's seared throat the contents of a bottle of cylinder oil that had been warming on the boiler head. The nauseous warm oil produced the desired results and "Cap" Collier remarks that the engineer distributed his internal economy over three or four miles of right-of-way and survived to pull many a drag of

pine logs in the years that followed.

Some logging road men were drifters, booming from camp to camp, while others home-guarded with one outfit and reared their children in the rough camps buried deep in the timber.

The bigger outfits often maintained a school in camp for the children of their employees and the following anecdote will illustrate the effect of camp life and explain why several generations of logging railroaders' offsprings followed their fathers along the twisting steel woods pikes. The teacher in camp asked one of the sons of an engineer a problem in arithmetic; "If you had twenty apples and gave Sally five and gave Bill six, how many apples would you have left?" Young Johnny pondered this for a time but could not arrive at a solution. The teacher thought that it might be easier if the question was phrased in terms more familiar to the lad, so she said, "Forget about the apples, John. Now, if they load forty cars of logs at Camp One today and Nelson brings out ten cars with his engine and Swanson brings out eight cars with his engine, how many cars will be left for your father's engine?"

Johnny mulled this over for a minute and replied, "Well, I don't know just exactly how many cars, but it will be every damn' pound the old Two-Spot can wiggle with!"

Life in the camps was never monotonous. Hunting and fishing were prime pastimes and dances were held that made up in gaiety for the lack of polish. The floor might be splintered by the calks of booted loggers and perhaps only an accordion or a fiddle provided the music, but there was laughter and light hearts under the glow of the kerosene lamps. The crews might be saddened by the loss of a brakie gone under the cars or an engine crew dropped to death through a weak trestle, but time healed the hurts and the trains went rolling on, from the rain forests of British Columbia to the redwood camps of California.

The red hell of forest fires might wipe out a camp but soon the snorting lokeys would be churning out of new locations while snags and stumps were still smouldering.

But even as the donkeys barked and cables smashed turns of logs through the underbrush, the lokeys were tracing "finis" with their smoke plumes tossed against the blue skies overhead Track and trestle work was costly, and the gas engine crept into the woods to spell death to most logging railroads. Crawler tractors bulldozed their own steep trails and logging trucks followed in their wake, free of the limitations of track. Today only a fraction of the vast mileage of logging pikes that traced a steel path through the western timberlands remain in operation. Steam power on these scattered survivors has largely been replaced by Diesel locomotives, robbing the timber industry of its most colorful action.

A few grizzled oldtimers who still chew "snoose" and wrestle kinked chokers remain in the big woods. Dozing on benches by the bunkhouse door on sunny Sunday mornings, they recall the old days, the rant and bark of the steam donkey, and they feel sorry for the crop of young loggers who never heard a Shay roar up a 4% grade or a Climax topped with a Radley-Hunter stack battle a switch-back, the string of laden bunks screeching flanges against rusty rails when God was in Heaven and Steam was King in the tall and uncut.

HOW HAVE THE MIGHTY FALLEN! This 4-4-0, bereft of her stave pilot, dreams of departed glory as she clanks along with a log train for the Algoma Lumber Company near Upper Klamath Lake, Oregon. Built by Baldwin in 1872, she was once a proud passenger engine bearing road number 15 on the Oregon & California Railroad. When this line was taken over by the Southern Pacific, the latter road assigned her number 1506, and later she was sold to the Algoma logging pike. Her former diet of neat billets of fir, cut in 2 foot lengths, has been supplanted by pine limbs as she humbly plods about her daily chores for the pine logging outfit. (Tecrasilk Photo, Grahame Hardy collection)

MOUNT HOOD RAILROAD COMPANY operated this two-truck woodburning Shay on their standard gauge logging operations. Numbered 1, she was named the BUD in honor of "Bud" Eccles, teen-aged son of one of the owners of the Oregon Lumber Company who controlled the Mount Hood road. Young Eccles met an awful death when he became entangled in the cable and drum of a donkey engine used for pulling lumber cars up an incline at Viento, Oregon, about 1900. Shown here with the geared locomotive are W. H. Eccles, in the cab; Ham Brightson, in the gangway; and S. M. Osborn, standing in the wood bin of the tank. (Courtesy of Arthur M. Sayre)

STEEL IN THE TIMBER. Humpbacked Shay locomotive, No. 2 of the Smith-Powers Logging Company, stands on track supported by pole cribbing while track gang lays steel on a new spur. Loggers have already delivered saw logs to the new rollway at the far right. Ties, rail, and angle bars for the construction project are loaded on the makeshift flat car behind the locomotive, formed by placing small logs on two sets of disconnected logging bunks.

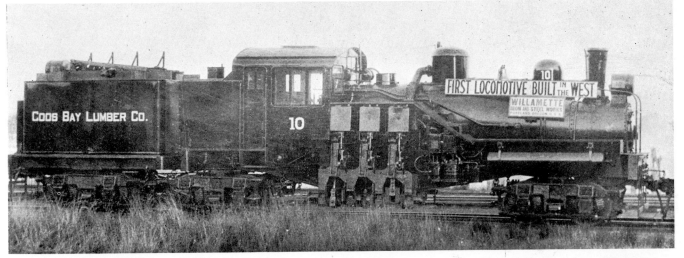

WILLAMETTE IRON & STEEL WORKS of Portland, Oregon, turned out their first Shay-type locomotive for the Coos Bay Lumber Company in 1922. The banner proclaiming "First Locomotive Built In The West" is in error, as California firms were turning out locomotives in the 1860's. No. 10, a 3-truck Shay design, was a success only after her original cylinders were recast, but she was followed by a number of very satisfactory geared engines from Willamette's shops, one or two of them still at work in the Oregon woods. (Courtesy of Mrs. M. P. Hughes)

HOME FROM THE TIMBER, the crew of loggers ride into camp behind the RATTLER on B. F. Brock's Mosquito & Coal Creek Railroad near Eufaula, in Washington's Cowlitz County. The RATTLER was a wood-burning 0-6-0 Baldwin saddle tank acquired by Brock in 1890. An auxiliary tender for hauling fuel is coupled behind her wooden cab. Oxen in large numbers were used in the woods of the Brock logging enterprise. (Courtesy of Vern Goe and John T. Labbe collection)

SMITH-POWERS LOGGING COMPANY operated several trim 2-8-2 types on their main line hauls in Coos County, Oregon. No. 101, a chunky Baldwin with neat striping, is shown shortly after her arrival in Marshfield. Trainmaster Dan Murphy is seated in the cab, with Fireman Georgie Taylor and Engineer Ed Mc-Carran on the ground. These standard gauge rod engines operated from Marshfield to Powers, Oregon, where geared engines took over for the steep climb into the Albert H. Powers logging camps. (Courtesy of Mrs. M. P. Hughes)

NORTHWEST TOOTHPICK. Logs from the Pacific Slope forests rode to the sawmills on disconnected trucks or "bunks", which could be strung out to accommodate loads of varying lengths. This type of equipment made the use of air brakes impossible and trains were controlled on descending grades by nimble-footed brakies who wielded iron "hickies" in place of the conventional wooden brake clubs. The equipment shown here belonged to the Bellingham Bay & Eastern, a pike operating in Northwestern Washington; the initials on the truck castings indicate Seattle, Lake Shore & Eastern Railroad ancestry. (Courtesy of Fred Jukes)

DEEP IN THE RAIN FOREST near Hoquiam, Washington, this three-domed Hinkley is at work on a logging railroad. Before being relegated to the timber pike, she is believed to have been a road engine used on the Oregon Railway & Navigation Company; although shorn of her graceful stave pilot, she retains her clerestory style of cab roof and bears the legend "Union Pacific", on her steam chest casting, a clue to her probable ancestry. Many engines from major roads, such as old No. 3, passed through the hands of equipment dealers and ended up on logging pikes, often losing their identity in the transactions. (Courtesy of Fred Jukes)

ON A NARROW LEDGE across the face of a sheer rock bluff, this three-truck Climax trundles her burden of logs in the northwest corner of Washington. This Kinsey photograph was taken on the English Logging Company operations at Camp 9; the lad straddling the headlight on the cab roof is Alvin G. Tate, member of a large family of logging railroad enginemen. (Courtesy of Jack Slattery, Jack's Photo Service)

FORKS LOGGING COMPANY'S No. 2, a Climax geared locomotive, pops off in Washington's big timber for the benefit of pioneer Northwest logging photographer Darius Kinsey. The log snubbed to her pilot is being skidded along between the rails, a method frequently used on logging pikes where the steep grades made the use of cars unfeasible. When the dense undergrowth became tinder-dry in hot weather, just one spark was necessary to turn the heavy stands of timber into a roaring inferno; note the screen bonnet on the diamond stack to help prevent forest fires. (Darius Kinsey photo, collection of Jesse E. Ebert, Seattle, Washington, courtesy of Ralph W. Andrews)

NOVEL SPARK ARRESTER of unusual design was applied to Engine No. 8 of the Sunset Logging Company. This logging railway connected with the trackage of the Southern Pacific at Hurlburt, Oregon, near the old Timber station on the former Pacific Railway & Navigation Co. line. The man standing in front of this two-truck Shay is Herbert Arey, veteran Southern Pacific engineer who came west off the Boston & Maine. Now deceased, Mr. Arey was noted for his excellent railroad photography and his skill as an engineman. (H. L. Arey photo, courtesy of Fred Jukes)

HEADED FOR THE BIG TIMBER, this 3-truck Shay with a diamond stack is shown in Portland, Oregon. She belonged to a Washington logging line, the Newaukum Valley Railroad, where she was numbered 2. The geared mountain climber was built in Lima, Ohio, by the Lima Locomotive & Machine Company. Engines such as old No. 2 were the workhorses of the big woods. (Angelus Studio photograph)

Along the iron pike to glory went the brass-bound locomotives and their trains of wooden cars. Whether rambling across the burning deserts or climbing the cool mountain heights, the sight and sound of their passing endeared them to all who loved speed, grace, motion, and the lingering aroma of steam and hot valve oil. The fragrant woodsmoke no longer trails over the rocky hillside where the tracks cling to the ledge high above the brawling stream, but the memories are ever green.

Let this be a tribute to the Iron Horse and the men who rode him proudly into the pages of history on the burnished rails of the Pacific Slope. (Southern Pacific photo)